DEATH PENALTY

IN A NUTSHELL

THIRD EDITION

By

VICTOR STREIB

Professor of Law
Ohio Northern University
Visiting Professor of Law
Elon University

THOMSON

WEST

Mat #40699860

Thomson/West have created this publication to provide you with accurate and authoritative information concerning the subject matter covered. However, this publication was not necessarily prepared by persons licensed to practice law in a particular jurisdiction. Thomson/West are not engaged in rendering legal or other professional advice, and this publication is not a substitute for the advice of an attorney. If you require legal or other expert advice, you should seek the services of a competent attorney or other professional.

Nutshell Series, In a Nutshell, the Nutshell Logo and West Group are trademarks registered in the U.S. Patent and Trademark Office.

© West, a Thomson business, 2003, 2005
© 2008 Thomson/West
        610 Opperman Drive
        St. Paul, MN 55123
        1–800–313–9378

Printed in the United States of America

ISBN: 978–0–314–18982–0

TEXT IS PRINTED ON 10% POST
CONSUMER RECYCLED PAPER

To
Lynn,
and to
Jessi and Noah

*

PREFACE

What could be more dramatic and demanding for a lawyer or any other criminal justice professional than a death penalty case? In the field of criminal law, these are the worst crimes committed by the worst offenders. In criminal procedure, these are the most complicated cases. In our day-to-day lives, these are the cases that make the headlines and provide the storyline for our movies and murder mysteries. This Nutshell explains the law and legal process followed in these truly extraordinary cases.

This brief text is designed to serve several purposes. The first audience is made up of law students, particularly those taking a course on death penalty law and practice. It is written intentionally to be in sync with nationally published cases and materials on this topic and to serve as brief sketch of almost all of the issues covered in those large and detailed texts. Another part of this law student audience includes those doing research and/or writing a paper on a death penalty issue. This brief text will provide them a concise summary of their topic and place it in the broad context of death penalty law and procedure.

In addition to law students, this text is designed for practicing lawyers and other criminal justice professionals who find themselves involved in a death penalty case. Almost every unique death penalty issue they will confront is covered briefly in this text, with citations to the primary authorities they should consult. Another audience for this Nutshell comprises graduate students and upper-level undergraduate students studying the death penalty in criminology, criminal justice, or a related department. This brief text is written by a law professor/death penalty lawyer primarily for law students and other lawyers, so the language may be less familiar to nonlawyers but is still accessible. Last, but certainly not least, the educated general public will find this Nutshell to provide a complete, stem-to-stern description of the substantive and procedural law of the death penalty in the United States in the early 21st century. However, this is not another book about why the death penalty is or is not moral, or wise, or effective. The effort here is to provide a factual description of what death penalty law is and how it works, leaving to others the gnarly questions of whether we should have it at all.

This text is organized for use either as a progression from chapter to chapter, exploring all of death penalty law in a logical order, or as a brief source of specific information about a succinct issue within death penalty law. The first four chapters sketch the background and context of the death penalty, including the history, the basic constitutional issues, and the arguments for and against this ultimate punishment. The second major part of the book covers substantive criminal law topics. In addition to the specific crimes that carry with them the possibility of the death penalty, these chapters describe the additional factors that pull the jury toward a death sentence or push them toward a life sentence.

Parts Three and Four cover the complex, sometimes Byzantine procedures followed in death cases. On the premise that all of the players should know what happens at their own stage and at all of the other stages, these chapters run from arrest to execution. The operating theme is to describe only the unique way that death penalty cases are handled and not to go through all of the procedures of all criminal cases (99% of which are not death cases). Finally, Part Five collects several special death penalty issues for isolated consideration. These include the pivotal role of the capital defense attorney, the integral problems of bias in the system, and the specter of mistakenly executing the innocent. The final chapter explores foreign and international law in an effort to place the American death penalty system into a global context.

Every story gets a spin from the storyteller, so you should know about my background and perspective. I have taught criminal law topics since 1971 and capital punishment courses since 1987. I research and write about death penalty issues, particularly the death penalty for juveniles and for women. In addition to this work as a law professor, I serve as defense counsel for death row prisoners before courts all over the country. Having tried mightily (and undoubtedly failed) to present neutral and evenhanded descriptions, I suspect that my views unavoidably come through.

Every attempt has been made to keep the language in this text informal, but undoubtedly a good deal of "legaleze" has crept into it. One convention that should be pointed out is the fairly consistent use of the male pronoun when referring to a defendant in a death penalty case or a death row prisoner. It seemed to the author that this convention was most appropriate, given that around 99% of those persons are male. When other individuals within the death penalty system are referred to, the typical "he or she" terminology is used.

Finally, many thanks are in order to many people. The Ohio Northern University College of Law and Elon University School of Law have been generous in providing me time, space, funding and encouragement in this effort. My family has, as always, allowed me to slave away at the office, doing what I seemingly must do, instead of going on vacations and family outings like normal people. Far more important than their tolerance is their daily encouragement and support for my work, without which you would not be reading these words.

V.S.

Greensboro, NC
August 2008

OUTLINE

Page

**Chapter 4. Constitutional Parameters of
the Current Era Death Penalty** ------ 42
§ 4.1 Approving the Current Era Death Penalty System------------------------------------ 43
§ 4.2 Rejecting Mandatory Death Penalties -- 48
§ 4.3 Post–1976 Major Constitutional Rulings -- 51

PART II. SUBSTANTIVE CRIMINAL LAW ISSUES

Chapter 5. Defining Capital Crimes ------ 57
§ 5.1 Basic Premises of Crime and Punish-
ment--- 57
§ 5.2 Historical Evolution of Capital Crime
Category--------------------------------------- 62
§ 5.3 Narrowing to Murder in the Current
Era--- 66
§ 5.4 Re–Expanding Capital Crime Categories --- 71

**Chapter 6. Aggravating and Mitigating
Circumstances**-------------------------------- 72
§ 6.1 Requirements and Limitations----------- 73
§ 6.2 Common Aggravating Circumstances--- 81
§ 6.3 Common Mitigating Circumstances ----- 86
§ 6.4 Discriminatory Impact and Unintend-
ed Consequences--------------------------- 91

Chapter 7. Special Defenses ------------------ 97
§ 7.1 Insufficient Criminal Intent -------------- 97
§ 7.2 Below Minimum Age ----------------------- 100
§ 7.3 Mentally Retarded -------------------------- 103
§ 7.4 Legal Insanity ------------------------------- 106

PART III.   TRIAL–LEVEL PROCEDUR-AL ISSUES

PART IV. POST–TRIAL PROCEDURAL ISSUES

PART V. SPECIAL DEATH PENALTY ISSUES

OUTLINE

*

TABLE OF CASES

References are to Pages

A

B

C

O

P

R

S

T

DEATH PENALTY

IN A NUTSHELL

THIRD EDITION

*

PART I
BACKGROUND AND CONTEXT

CHAPTER 1

HISTORY AND EVOLUTION

Modern death penalty law is more the result of historical evolution than of compelling logic. This ultimate penalty dates back to the earliest periods of recorded history, and the American experience is simply the latest chapter. Therefore, knowledge of this historical context is necessary to understand current death penalty law.

§ 1.1   Pre–American Period

Any history of the world devotes substantial attention to the more prominent executions punctuating events over the centuries. Even a moment's reflection reveals that one of the most important and well-known events in recorded history was, at base, an execution. The crucifixion of Jesus of Nazareth launched a worldwide religious movement. However, with apologies to religious sensitivities, Jesus was a convicted criminal, lawfully sentenced

1

to death by the governmental authorities, and publicly executed for his crimes. The then-common instrument of his governmental execution—a cross—has become the universal symbol of Christianity, with huge examples towering over our cities and small examples hanging from chains around our necks. If this execution had occurred today, the symbol of Christianity might well be lethal injection's hypodermic needle instead of the cross.

But the death penalty far predates the crucifixion of Jesus. Beheading was the prescribed method of imposing the death penalty under the Ancient Laws of China. This gave us the term "capital" punishment as a euphemism for the death penalty, since the punishment literally beheaded or "decapitated" the offender. The axe was the instrument of capital punishment in early Egypt, Rome, Greece, and Assyria. While many other means of imposing death were used throughout the ages, the point here is that the death penalty has been authorized since the earliest days of civilization.

The death penalty went in and out of fashion, particularly in Western Europe, through the colonization of the new world. In this regard, the practice in England is particularly important, since so many of the American colonists were from England and the English common law is the foundation for American common law. In addition to the many common felons put to death for their garden-variety crimes, some of England's highest ranking individuals lost their heads for their transgressions: Duke of Somerset (1552), Lady Jane Grey (1554), Lord

Guildford Dudley (1554), Mary, Queen of Scots (1587), Sir Walter Raleigh (1618), Charles' I (1649), Lord William Russell (1683), and Simon, Lord Lovat (1747).

Many scholarly and general readership books, articles, films, drawings, and other accounts have described the more sensational and well-known executions inflicted by a wide variety of imaginative yet gruesome techniques. While beheading by axe, sword, or guillotine gave us the term "capital" punishment, governments also have executed prisoners throughout the centuries by flaying alive, boiling in oil, drawing, quartering and disemboweling, burning at the stake, and breaking on the wheel. The overarching goals seem to have been inflicting extreme pain and indignity, as well as death, upon the offender and to have made a public spectacle of the offender's death.

Despite an occasional outcry about the brutality of such executions, it is fair to say that the death penalty was alive and well in Western Europe and essentially around the world during the time period in which the American colonies were being formed and our early laws were being established. In fact, the death penalty in Western Europe survived until the middle of the 20th century, at which time it was abolished throughout the continent. England greatly limited the death penalty beginning in the late 19th century and completely abolished it in 1965.

§ 1.2   Colonial Period to 1970s

The land now claimed by the United States was originally populated by indigenous peoples for many centuries, but our recorded history of the death penalty essentially begins with European colonization. One of the many European practices brought to America by the colonists was the death penalty for a wide variety of crimes. As a result, the earliest American penal codes included the death penalty. With only minor variations on this theme, the death penalty has remained a part of our culture and our legal system since these earliest beginnings.

The first recorded execution within Europe's American colonies was of George Kendall in 1608. The first woman, Jane Champion, was executed in the Virginia colonies in 1632, and the first juvenile offender, 16–year-old Thomas Graunger, was executed in Plymouth Colony, Massachusetts in 1642. From these earliest days, approximately 20,000 executions have occurred. Our peak execution rates were in the 1930s, with the maximum being the 199 executions which occurred in 1935. This rate has not been matched since that time, with current annual execution rates being one fourth of the 1935 rate of 199 executions. In 2006, for example, we had 53 executions, and in 2007 we had only 42.

The early colonies in what is now northeastern United States gave the death penalty a restricted scope. By the late 18th century, capital crimes generally were limited to murder, a few other violent crimes, treason, and various acts of sodomy. In the geographical area that was to become the southern states, the death penalty was seen as instrumental in maintaining the institution of slavery. More generally, the death penalty took firmer roots in the southeast and has continued there through today much more strongly than in any other part of the United States, except for the unmatched leadership of Texas.

As the newly-formed United States grew and expanded westward, reliance upon the death penalty began to wane. Many states reduced the number of crimes for which the death penalty could be imposed, and, in 1846, Michigan became the first state to abolish the death penalty for all crimes except treason. About a dozen other states joined Michigan in the early 20th century. Across the United States, the death penalty became concentrated in the southeastern states, a pattern that has continued now into the 21st century.

The federal government has always had the death penalty for selected federal crimes, but death sentences and actual executions for federal crimes are rarely imposed, certainly as compared to those at the state level. This is even more true for military crimes, with almost all of these rare executions occurring during wartime.

The death penalty was used fairly aggressively in the 1920s and 1930s, with violent crime and high-profile executions sharing the front page. Very little evolution could be seen specifically in the statutes or case law, however, and death penalty law continued pretty much the same through the 1950s. Almost all executions in the north and west were for murder, but the southeastern states continued to execute offenders also for rape (almost all black male offenders with white female victims), as well as for robbery and other crimes.

The major change came from a lessening of public and political support for the death penalty during the 1950s and 1960s. Although very little changed officially through the courts or legislatures, actual executions dwindled and then stopped altogether. Colorado's execution of Louis Monge in 1967 was to be the last execution in this country for a decade. Many observers assumed that the United States was quietly phasing out the death penalty, as had been done in England and the rest of Western Europe during this time period.

§ 1.3 Current Death Penalty Era

A common error in descriptions of the modern death penalty system is the premise that the current era began with the holding of the Supreme Court in *Gregg v. Georgia*, 428 U.S. 153, 96 S.Ct. 2909, 49 L.Ed.2d 859 (1976). While *Gregg* did mark the Supreme Court's first opportunity in the current era to rule that the death penalty in general was not Cruel and Unusual Punishment as that concept is defined by the 8th Amendment to the United States Constitution, *Gregg* was decided several years after the actual beginning of the era of the modern death penalty system. The operating premise is that the death penalty system begins when a capital crime is committed, the crime is investigated and the apparent offender is arrested.

The trial typically follows at least a year after arrest, and subsequent appellate and post-conviction challenges extend on for many years. Actual execution, if it ever occurs, takes place typically about ten years after the death sentence is imposed.

The previous death penalty era was terminated by the Supreme Court's decision in *Furman v. Georgia*, 408 U.S. 238, 92 S.Ct. 2726, 33 L.Ed.2d 346 (1972), which in effect struck down all then-existing death penalty statutes. However, both Florida and Utah enacted new death penalty statutes before the end of 1972, and 15 more states followed suit in 1973. By the date of the *Gregg* decision (July 2, 1976), at least 35 states and the federal government had enacted new death penalty statutes. Demonstrating the resolve of these death penalty states, more than 460 capital offenders had already been sentenced to death under these new death penalty statutes by early 1976. The current era death penalty system clearly was already functioning and obviously had not waited for the *Gregg* decision by the Supreme Court.

Therefore, the origins of the current death penalty era can be found in the months following the Supreme Court's decision in *Furman* on June 29, 1972. For simplicity of comparison, this analysis marks the beginning as 1973, allowing for a period of six months following *Furman* for the various jurisdictions to reconsider the death penalty. Fairly comprehensive data are available through the end of 2007 as of this writing, even though the current death penalty era continues for the foreseeable future. These 35 years from 1973 through 2007 represent a halting progression through an early shaping period into what is now a fully mature death penalty system, albeit one under reconsideration from several perspectives.

Actual executions began soon after the *Gregg* decision, with the first being that of Gary Mark Gilmore on Jan. 17, 1977, in Utah. By the end of 2007, 1,099 persons had been executed in this current era by 32 states and the federal government, with the continuing execution rate varying between 50 and 70 persons per year. Texas is by far the leader in this practice, accounting for 41% of all American executions since 1977. Well over three-quarters of these 1,099 executions have occurred in the southeastern states.

As of the end of 2007, a total of 36 states have death penalty statutes in force. The federal government has two death penalty statutes, one applying to crimes by members of the military and the other applying to nonmilitary crimes. Fourteen states and the District of Columbia do not have the death penalty. These abolitionist states are located primarily in New England and in the upper Midwest. However, even among the 38 official death penalty jurisdictions, the amount of actual death sentences and executions varies extremely. At the end of 2007, a total of 3,309 prisoners were on these 38 death rows.

CHAPTER 2

ARGUMENTS FOR AND AGAINST THE DEATH PENALTY

The centuries-old debate over the death penalty typically dwells on theoretical, philosophical and religious pros and cons. However, the issues that arise in the day-to-day operations of the American death penalty system often encompass less lofty but perhaps more troubling concerns. The fundamental question here is not whether certain crimes and certain offenders deserve the death penalty. Rather, it is whether we can trust a hodgepodge of loosely-connected government agencies to carry out the death penalty in a fair and rational manner. Sadly, the experience in the United States, as elsewhere, has been that huge, expensive government programs seldom accomplish their perhaps worthy goals, due in large part to the problems that plague our entire society. Following is a sketch of the most common arguments for and against the death penalty, both within criminological and religious theory and within the day-to-day death penalty system actually operating in the real world.

§ 2.1   Retribution and Symbolism

Undoubtedly the most significant and pervasive justification for the American death penalty is retribution. The horrible murders for which death can be imposed are so shocking as to inflame strong passions to strike back, to make the murderer suffer as the victims suffered. Almost without fail, prosecuting attorneys in death penalty cases consult the murder victim's friends and family as to what punishment they desire for the offender. Not surprisingly, the family's extreme grief and anger typically cause them to urge the death penalty. This all-too-human passion is simply a desire for revenge against the person who has wreaked such horrible harm on their friend or family member.

The other, loftier meaning of retribution is "justice" or "just desserts," essentially, whether one who kills "deserves" to die himself? This argument often stems from a fundamental religious perspective, such as "an eye for an eye." The notion of a "life for a life" can be found in a wide variety of religions and religious texts, although most major religions today do not condone the death penalty in general. Nonetheless, many pro-death penalty advocates rely very strongly upon this concept of "justice" for the condemned murderer.

Retribution, however defined, has always been a key part of the foundation of our criminal justice system, not just in the area of the death penalty. Decisions made by legislators, judges, and jurors often rely explicitly or implicitly upon retribution as the justification for their actions. The Supreme Court has held that retribution is one of several acceptable bases for the death penalty, although some of the Justices thought that basing legal punishments upon retribution is beneath the dignity of the law. Gregg v. Georgia, 428 U.S. 153, 96 S.Ct. 2909, 49 L.Ed.2d 859 (1976).

Death penalty opponents have provided several responses to these retribution arguments. First, some question whether the victim's friends and family constitute the most appropriate group of persons to make this life-or-death decision. Such a group typically includes persons absolutely devastated by the victim's murder, to the point of being at least extremely emotional and probably somewhat irrational. As sympathetic as we are to such distraught individuals, it is not clear that persons in that state of mind should be making governmental and public policy decisions of such significance. Indeed, the American criminal justice system is based on a premise of decision-making by calm, rational professionals, so incorporating the highly emotional opinions of the victim's family is counter to that premise.

A corollary to the above argument addresses the now-common practice of criminal prosecutors to include the recommendation of the victim's family in deciding whether to seek the death penalty. Some jurisdictions even permit a representative of the victim's family to sit at the prosecution's table during trial, as if they are the clients of the prosecuting attorneys. However, this practice blurs a basic difference between a murder case in criminal law and a wrongful death case in tort law. In the latter, the plaintiff's attorney clearly does represent the aggrieved family and is seeking compensation for their loss and for their pain and suffering. However, in a murder case in criminal court, the prosecuting attorney represents the state or federal government and all of the citizens of that jurisdiction. A criminal prosecutor's sworn oath is to seek justice for all of the people, not just retribution for the victim's family.

The rationale of "an eye for an eye" does lend itself to a sense of balance, of tit for tat. The offender who takes a life should have his life taken. However, literally making the punishment fit the crime is not found in any other area of criminal law. The car thief is not punished by having his car stolen, the battering husband is not himself battered by the police, and the bank embezzler does not in turn have her bank accounts defrauded. In this literal sense, the punishment is almost never like the crime, so the push for taking the life of the killer seems out of context with the rest of criminal law.

Those who oppose this rationale point out that only about 1% of all convicted killers are actually executed, with the rest serving various prison sentences. Therefore, it appears society has concluded that 99% of killers do not "deserve" to die. Even if we doubled or tripled the number of executions, we still would not be executing $95+\%$ of all killers. Therefore, almost all convicted killers apparently do not fit the "eye for an eye" formula.

One last version of this "eye for an eye" rationale is that the offender should suffer the same fate as the victim. The offender didn't consider the victim's life to be of value and concern, so we should treat the offender as he treated the victim. Opponents to this rationale point out that the murder of the victim was the act of a murderer. A murderer, almost by definition, does not display thoughtfulness, morality, and rationality in his decision to take a life. As society debates and deliberates this life-or-death decision of whether to take a life, it seems odd for society to look to the personal standards of murderers for guidance as to how we should act. Most would agree that society's standards should be considerably loftier than the standards of murderers and would reject any societal deference to the murderer's level of concern for the victim's life.

While not a classic justification for criminal punishment, the notion of symbolism plays a major role in American death penalty law. As a society, we are outraged at our overall murder rate and determined to make a clear statement about it. Our most prominent statement may be to declare that these crimes are so outrageous as to qualify those who commit them for death at the hands of the state. Whether or not such executions are ever imposed or actually carried out, society has thereby made its values known in the most extreme of measures. Such symbolism also occurs on an individual case basis. A homicide victim's family and local community typically express disappointment if the death penalty is not sought or obtained in their individual case, somehow equating the severity of the penalty with a societal judgment as to the inherent value of their victim's life.

The other side of this issue includes the notion that our symbolic statements should not demean the value of human life or fall beneath the dignity of the law. At the individual case level, opponents argue that the criminal sentencing process is not designed generally to assess the value of the victim's life to the family and community. They also note that executing the killer cannot bring back the victim or provide any lasting comfort to anyone. Moreover, to the degree that any members of the victim's family or the community demand the death of the offender as an essential salve for their wounds, opponents simply suggest that this is too extreme and that no form of punishment of the offender would be sufficient to heal their wounds.

§ 2.2   Incapacitation and Deterrence

A very common and seemingly logical justification given by those who support the death penalty is that executing this convicted murderer will reduce the number of future murders. Any criminal sanction which promises to prevent future crime is very attractive, and this argument claims the ultimate benefit: saving innocent lives. Unlike retribution's somewhat unsavory taste for some, the prevention argument appeals to everyone.

One basic mode of preventing future crimes is to take away the present offender's ability to commit them through incapacitation. This logic has lead to cutting off the hands of pickpockets, castrating rapists, and disbarring lawyers who steal from their clients. This approach is referred to as incapacitating or restraining the offender, preventing him or her from committing that particular crime at least for a given period of time. The focus of incapacitation is solely upon the future behavior of this specific offender and not upon other potential offenders of a like mind.

Incapacitation is not the same principle as specific deterrence. The latter presumes punishing a past offender sufficiently will convince him to avoid repeating his criminal conduct in the future, not because he can't do it but because he fears more of the detested punishment if he does. Incapacitation, in contrast, makes it essentially impossible for the offender to repeat his crimes, not because he fears more punishment but because he is physically unable to commit the crimes.

The death penalty serves incapacitation, not specific deterrence. Obviously, a foolproof means of physically preventing a specific killer from ever killing again is to take his life. An executed homicide offender will never kill again. Incapacitation is the one justification that the death penalty serves better than could any other criminal punishment.

Death penalty opponents note that other than the extremely small chance of escape from prison, an imprisoned murderer also is incapacitated, essentially permanently, from committing any murders outside the confines of prison. Therefore, it may be that long term imprisonment is nearly as effective an incapacitant as is the death penalty. In any event, research reveals that murderers are very unlikely to repeat their crimes, so the overall need for a long term incapacitant is unclear.

In addition to incapacitating the executed offender, death penalty proponents argue that its use will deter the behavior of others. The rationale of this principle of general deterrence is that others who were considering committing murders will be frightened away from that behavior due to the threat of being executed for those murders. The appeal of this principle is that it is basically intuitive; a credible threat of being killed if you do something arguably would make anyone think twice before doing it. General deterrence is very popular in political campaigns as well, with almost all political candidates espousing their personal belief that the death penalty is a deterrent.

This general deterrence principle assumes, of course, such things as (1) your knowledge of the death penalty's existence, (2) your belief that you will be caught and convicted for your acts, (3) your calculation that you would be within the 1% of convicted killers who are actually executed, and (4) your engaging in this detailed cost/benefit analysis before you pull the trigger. Here is where this seductive theory breaks down in practice. An enormous amount of academic research has been performed around this thesis, and the results are as clear as any in social science can be. The death penalty is no greater general deterrent of the behavior of other potential murderers than is long term imprisonment. It appears that most murderers don't tend to think before they act, plus they have an unrealistic view of their ability to escape arrest and conviction. In any event, fear of spending the rest of one's life in prison seems more than sufficient to provide the deterrent effect needed.

Some empirical research on this phenomenon has found that the murder rate goes up, not down, following an execution. This finding, dubbed the "brutalization effect," is essentially that the death penalty stimulates more murders than otherwise would occur. The common explanation for the unexpected result is that the death penalty "brutalizes" the surrounding community, both diminishing respect for life in general and providing the unfortunate example of our highest leaders in public office intentionally taking a person's life. In any event, despite the professed claims of American political leaders, these research findings indicate that the death penalty does not actually serve a general deterrent function and apparently has the opposite effect.

§ 2.3 Bias, Caprice, and Error

Many of the divisions between the pro-death penalty and anti-death penalty camps can be explained by their different perspectives. Pro-death penalty groups tend to focus upon who "deserves" to die from a religious and philosophical perspective, with few if any advocates giving serious consideration to the glaring differences between death penalty theory and actual practice. Anti-death penalty groups tend to focus more upon the serious malfunctions of the real-world death penalty system. Both groups oppose bias, caprice, and error in the imposition of the death penalty, but theoretical discussions tend to be much purer than the actions and decisions of the real world of criminal justice.

A key fact from the real world is that less than 1% of those who commit homicide are actually executed for their crimes. Regardless of the constant drumbeat of media coverage of death penalty issues, the reality is that we almost never actually use it. If, in fact, this ultimate punishment is to be reserved for only the most egregious cases, then one would expect those cases to be limited to mass murderers, serial murderers, repeat murderers, etc. However, the hapless few who actually get executed are not the "worst of the worst" of all of killers. They tend to be a fairly random selection from all those arrested for homicide, but a selection skewed by race, sex, poverty level, and just the luck of the draw as to who has been their judge, jury, and defense counsel.

Discrimination is one of the most obvious problems. Research reveals clear and unabashed discrimination based upon race of offender and race of victim. That is, black offenders who kill white victims are several times more likely to be sentenced to death than white offenders who kill black victims under similar circumstances. Research during the past two decades documents that the major racial factor is race of victim. Nothing in American statutes or case law instructs us to treat the murder of a white victim more seriously than the murder of a black victim, but this is in fact what happens at every stage of the process. Try as we might, race discrimination in the application of the death penalty and throughout the criminal justice system continues to stain our efforts to maintain a fair and evenhanded process.

The death penalty system discriminates even more sharply on the basis of sex of offender, with women almost totally excluded. Part of this gender differential can be explained by the different kinds of homicide committed by women as compared to those committed by men, but a residue of gender bias appears to remain. At bottom, despite the well-documented daily violence against women perpetrated mostly by men, it appears that we are less willing to subject women than men to the death penalty.

Poverty level of the offender and victim also determines in part the outcome. That is, an offender from lower economic and social strata who murders a victim from higher economic and social strata stands the greatest chance of being sentenced to death and actually executed. These and other legally irrelevant factors cause these literally life-and-death decisions to be made in a pervasively discriminatory manner.

Perhaps even more bedeviling than the impact of these various forms of discrimination is the appearance of mere chance and caprice. Comparing sketches of the crimes and criminals receiving the death penalty with those which receive only prison sentences, it seems impossible to find rational distinctions between the two lists. Many of what seem to be the worst cases end up with prison sentences, while many mid-level, garden-variety homicides receive the death penalty.

A major part of this apparent chance and caprice is the luck of the draw. Each capital jury is different, with some juries clearly leaning more toward the death penalty than other juries. Prosecuting attorneys have similar differences as to their interest in the death penalty. Even the same individual prosecutor may see political advantage in seeking the death penalty in one case while not in a nearly identical case falling at a different point in the political term of office. Judges also must keep one eye on the political polls if they face reelection, with several well-known examples of judges facing stiff political opposition for their decisions in death penalty cases. And as one moves around within almost any death penalty state, one can find hot spots and cold spots as to the actual imposition of the death penalty, even though the state law is supposed to be uniform across the entire state.

Probably the most important factor in caprice is the defense attorney for the capital defendant. While the 6th Amendment guarantees the "assistance of counsel," the ability, support-level, and work ethic of capital defense counsel vary quite widely. A capital defendant's attorney should be experienced in capital cases, should devote major portions of time and energy to the case, and be aided and supported by legal assistants, investigators, mitigation specialists, and other members of a complete defense team. This is the sort of team effort that the prosecuting attorney has, so the defense attorney should have a comparable team.

Only very rarely, however, does the defense team equal the prosecution team in numbers, experience, and funding. Most pro-death penalty advocates have no wish for the defendant to have inadequate counsel, although some have voiced criticisms of defense teams that "try too hard" to avoid the death penalty for their client. Anti-death penalty advocates regularly claim that the mismatch between prosecution and defense too often results in a denial of a full and fair consideration of the defendant's guilt and sentence. Capital defendants with inadequate defense teams may receive the death penalty while essentially identical cases result only in a prison sentence, with the only difference being the quality of the defense attorney.

The ultimate end result of discrimination, caprice, and just plain bad luck can be clear error: convicting and sentencing to death an innocent offender. The death penalty system is operated and controlled by human beings who are not immune to human error. Innocent people are sentenced to death and, in some cases, actually executed. Whether for or against the death penalty, almost no one wants innocent people executed. First is the obvious tragedy of the death of an innocent person, but remember that this also means that the real murderer is still running around loose with no one looking for him.

Over 125 innocent persons have been sent to death row in the current era (since 1973), and states such as Illinois have put a hold on executions to find out why. Several other states have also ordered a moratorium on executions. This criticism of the death penalty system may be the most telling politically, and many groups are studying means for improving the accuracy of the system and reducing the number of innocent persons receiving the death penalty. Some death penalty opponents are demanding perfect accuracy before executions can be carried out, but this is simply impossible to achieve. A system operated by human beings operating under intense political pressures is bound to make mistakes, so the more reasonable goal may be to minimize errors rather than to eliminate them. The overarching issue, of course, is how many death penalties for innocent persons is too many?

§ 2.4 Other Concerns

A wide variety of other, perhaps lesser, concerns exist for many people. One broad fear is the continuation of the cycle of violence by our killing those who have killed others. This is the ultimate legitimization of intentional, premeditated killings, a lesson that is not lost on young and impressionable persons wondering whether "thou shalt not kill" means what it says. Pro-death penalty advocates argue that a convicted murderer's life is not of comparable value as that of the innocent victim, and the only way to show proper respect for the victim's life is to impose the ultimate penalty upon the murderer who took that life. Death penalty opponents see all human life as being of infinite value, and the life-for-a-life premise of the death penalty simply continues the cycle of killing.

This cycle of violence debate is part of a larger concern about the nature of human dignity. Death, obviously, is inevitable, so executing a convicted murderer simply moves his death to a time somewhat earlier than it otherwise would have occurred. In essence, the death penalty does not require a life-or-death decision, it only imposes an "unnatural" death now in lieu of a "natural" death whenever nature takes its course. Life, at least life forever, is not an earthly option. Death penalty opponents, however, argue that the inevitability of death does not justify the government's imposition of an "early" death on a convicted offender.

The only major justification for criminal punishment in general that is not commonly given for the death penalty is reform of the offender. Obviously, in death penalty cases the offender is to be executed instead of being given a lengthy opportunity to reform himself. Note, however, the well-established tradition of permitting the condemned prisoner ample opportunity to consult with a religious advisor, typically a Catholic priest or Protestant minister, as execution draws near. Such religious counseling is made available even to those condemned prisoners who previously have shown no interest in religion. This suggests at least some governmental recognition of the prisoner's need to reform himself before leaving this life. Death penalty opponents nonetheless decry the condemned prisoner's lost opportunity to engage in fundamental reform and go on to lead a life of meaning and value.

At the other end of the spectrum from the value and meaning of human life, an often-heard argument for executing the offender is that it saves us the cost of providing room and board in a maximum security facility for the rest of the offender's life. Given the life expectancy of such prisoners and the annual costs of operating our prisons, the total expenditure might well be in the range of a million dollars.

The surprising fact is that the death penalty is much more expensive than life imprisonment. The very long and tedious death penalty process, coupled with the rarity of it ending in actual execution, results in a very high cost-per-execution. Research in several jurisdictions has shown that the average cost-per-execution is several million dollars, much more than the cost of keeping that executed prisoner in prison for several lifetimes. This is counterintuitive to those who argue that we shouldn't use precious tax dollars to feed and house convicted murderers. It turns out that many more of those tax dollars are required to execute the prisoner than would be needed to keep him in prison.

Another argument over the death penalty stems from the worldwide movement to abolish it. Essentially all developed nations with very much in common with the United States have abandoned the death penalty for domestic crimes, retaining it perhaps only for treason and war crimes. Among those countries still executing prisoners, China and Iran tend to be the perennial leaders. These are not countries which we tend to emulate in human rights matters. In addition, several international treaties forbid the application of the death penalty against juveniles, for example. Our stubborn refusal to abandon the juvenile death penalty until the Supreme Court found it unconstitutional in *Roper v. Simmons*, 543 U.S. 551, 125 S.Ct. 1183, 161 L.Ed.2d 1 (2005) had put the United States in conflict with this international law. The resulting domestic debate was whether we should be persuaded to join the rest of the global community or just continue to do what we think is best, even if we go it alone.

One final point of contention is both of immediate impact and of long term significance. Advocates of the death penalty point with great concern at violent crime in America, particularly our murder rate. We want answers, not theories, and we want them now. The death penalty is promised by some as the answer to murder, so it tends to be embraced by much of our society. This strong, emotional need for a ''quick fix'' for violent crime explains at least part of America's strong faith in the death penalty despite so many rational and factual questions concerning it.

Opponents of the death penalty point out that we are latching onto a "quick fix" for the extremely complex problem of violent crime. We might be compared to obese persons who grab at any new weight-loss program promising minimal if any effort on our part. We know in the back of our minds that the probable solution to our weight problem includes regular exercise and a careful diet, but these seem too daunting for us. Similarly, strong reliance upon the death penalty may divert us from seeking appropriate, long-term solutions to our violent crime problems. The "exercise and diet" alternative here requires us to face several of society's toughest problems, and they also seem too difficult for us to accomplish. However, our reliance upon the death penalty "quick fix" for our violent crime problem diverts us from a sober and realistic approach based upon facts and logic.

CHAPTER 3

BASIC CONSTITUTIONAL CHALLENGES AND LIMITATIONS

The bedrock of the American death penalty is the United States Constitution, guaranteeing Due Process and Equal Protection within the criminal justice system and prohibiting Cruel and Unusual Punishments by that system. Not surprisingly, these constitutional guarantees have channeled the application of the death penalty to specific crimes and offenders. Understanding these constitutional principles is critical to decoding death penalty law. Adding to the challenge is the fact that the Supreme Court has consistently held that these constitutional principles can and do "evolve" over time. Particularly since the early 1970s, even the most basic constitutional challenges and limitations have "evolved" dramatically and have changed the landscape of death penalty law.

§ 3.1 Critical Provisions of the United States Constitution

About 99% of death penalty cases are state prosecutions alleging violations of state law, being tried in state courts, and seeking to impose the state death penalty. Each state has its own constitution, and a state case must follow the provisions and requirements of that state's constitution. This nutshell does not deal directly with the statutes and constitutional provisions of each death penalty jurisdiction. Typically, death penalty states have death penalty practice manuals, prepared by the state attorney general, the state public defender, and/or a bar-related group and laying out the specific constitutional issues in those states.

Such state constitutional provisions can be instrumental in determining the outcome of a state death penalty case, and the state materials should be consulted in each case. Thankfully for the student of the overall American death penalty system, the state constitutional provisions of the death penalty states tend to be quite similar and can be spoken of in general terms. Each state constitution, for example, requires Due Process and prohibits cruel and/or unusual punishment in its own state death penalty system. The concept of what constitutes a fair process or a cruel punishment evolves over time, so an individual state's experiences with those concepts are relevant to determining death penalty cases in that specific state.

The most obvious provision of the United States Constitution that applies expressly to state death penalty systems is the 14th Amendment: "No State shall ... deprive any person of life, liberty, or property, without due process of law; nor deny to any person within its jurisdiction the equal protection of the laws." The first clause guaranteeing Due Process appears to run the gamut of criminal punishments. Any deprivation of life (death penalty), liberty (incarceration), or property (fine) must be based upon a system that is fundamentally fair and thus affords "Due Process" to the defendant. The 5th Amendment places a similar Due Process requirement on the federal criminal justice system.

The express language of the 5th and 14th Amendments anticipates that a state *can* impose the death penalty or "deprive any person of life," so long as the Due Process requirement is met. If the deprivation of life were not an acceptable option when these Amendments were written, then presumably no fairness requirement would have been imposed upon it. However, it seems equally clear that these Due Process provisions do not provide constitutional authorization for the death penalty or for any other form of criminal sanction. History, nonetheless, tells us that the death penalty was a fairly common punishment included in criminal laws at that time, so we can assume that the 5th and 14th Amendments simply intended to require Due Process or fairness whenever a federal or state criminal justice system sought to impose the death penalty.

The 14th Amendment also requires the states to provide "the equal protection of the laws" to all criminal defendants, including capital defendants. This Equal Protection provision obviously prohibits differential treatment of men and women or blacks and whites under death penalty laws and procedures. Equal Protection arguments also are made on behalf of poor defendants seeking what rich defendants have, such as skilled defense attorneys, expert witnesses, and mitigation specialists. Of course, such valuable defense team members cost money, and they typically must be paid from public funds if the defendant cannot afford to pay them.

The Supreme Court has struggled mightily to determine what minimum provisions must be made at state expense, fully recognizing that the most expensive, top of the line provisions are simply beyond the means of public funds to provide. Therefore, even the poorest capital defendant is appointed a defense attorney, with a growing number of states requiring that appointed counsel be particularly experienced and well-qualified in capital cases. However, almost never is the poor capital defendant represented by a group of the most competent (and most expensive) criminal lawyers, supported by a team of experts, investigators, and assistants, which might well be representing the rich capital defendant. As it turns out, the rich live quite differently than do the poor, even when facing death.

In contrast to the 14th Amendment's express limitations upon state capital cases, the key protections for criminal defendants in the United States Constitution's Bill of Rights are directed solely at the federal criminal justice system. *Barron v. Baltimore*, 32 U.S. 243, 7 Pet. 243, 8 L.Ed. 672 (1833). However, as a result of several sweeping Supreme Court decisions defining the content of 14th Amendment Due Process, almost all of these federal defendants' rights apply equally to all state governments. This means that capital defendants in state cases also receive, for example, the federal right against unreasonable searches and seizures found in the 4th Amendment. *Mapp v. Ohio*, 367 U.S. 643, 81 S.Ct. 1684, 6 L.Ed.2d 1081 (1961). State defendants also are protected by the 5th Amendment right not to be compelled to be a witness against yourself. *Miranda v. Arizona*, 384 U.S. 436, 86 S.Ct. 1602, 16 L.Ed.2d 694 (1966). The 6th Amendment's rights to a jury trial and to the assistance of defense counsel for federal defendants also have been extended to state defendants. *Duncan v. State of Louisiana*, 391 U.S. 145, 88 S.Ct. 1444, 20 L.Ed.2d 491 (1968); *Gideon v. Wainwright*, 372 U.S. 335, 83 S.Ct. 792, 9 L.Ed.2d 799 (1963).

More central to the death penalty issue, the 8th Amendment prohibits cruel and unusual punishments, as well as excessive bail and excessive fines. These latter two 8th Amendment rights, surprisingly, are among the very few federal constitutional rights not imposed upon the states by the Supreme Court through the 14th Amendment, but the Cruel and Unusual Punishment prohibition has been used in a similar manner. *Robinson v. California*, 370 U.S. 660, 82 S.Ct. 1417, 8 L.Ed.2d 758 (1962); *Furman v. Georgia*, 408 U.S. 238, 92 S.Ct. 2726, 33 L.Ed.2d 346 (1972). If cruel and unusual punishments are the focuses of concern, one would expect the death penalty to be at the center of that constitutional inquiry. The death penalty is seen by the Supreme Court as the ultimate criminal sanction, more severe than any other sanction permitted under American law, so 8th Amendment policy and analysis typically begin with that punishment.

This 8th Amendment issue presents a moving target for the courts and legislatures to address. The opening premise is that the death penalty was fairly common in American law when the 8th Amendment language was written. Therefore, it seems accepted that the death penalty was not cruel and unusual at the outset of 8th Amendment jurisprudence. *Furman v. Georgia*, 408 U.S. 238, 92 S.Ct. 2726, 33 L.Ed.2d 346 (Burger, C.J., dissenting) (1972). The death penalty was imposed for a wide variety of crimes in addition to murder and, for example, was suffered by children as well as by adults. *Coker v. Georgia*, 433 U.S. 584, 97 S.Ct. 2861, 53 L.Ed.2d 982 (1977); *Stanford v. Kentucky*, 492 U.S. 361, 109 S.Ct. 2969, 106 L.Ed.2d 306 (1989). If what it means to be a cruel and unusual punishment had remained fixed over the past two centuries, this would still be the law.

One of the most significant strengths of the United States Constitution, however, is that it changes over time, primarily through interpretation by the Supreme Court. The expected changes in 8th Amendment law were recognized in *Weems v. United States*, 217 U.S. 349, 30 S.Ct. 544, 54 L.Ed. 793 (1910). The 8th Amendment's prohibition of cruel and unusual punishments, according to *Weems*, "is not fastened to the obsolete but may acquire meaning as public opinion becomes enlightened by a humane justice." The Supreme Court revisited this concept half a century later in *Trop v. Dulles*, 356 U.S. 86, 78 S.Ct. 590, 2 L.Ed.2d 630 (1958). Chief Justice Warren's plurality opinion in *Trop* ex-

plained that the concept of cruel and unusual punishment under the 8th Amendment "must draw its
meaning from the evolving standards of decency
that mark the progress of a maturing society."
Under current cases, getting a clear fix on these
"evolving standards" as "enlightened by a humane
justice" both enables and bedevils the continuing
debate over the constitutionality of the death penalty in the 21st century.

The common assumption is any evolution of
standards of decency would move in the direction
of narrowing applications of the death penalty, but
such an arguably enlightened and merciful evolution is not certain. The current era has seen Supreme Court rulings that 8th Amendment standards have evolved beyond imposing the death
penalty for the crime of rape or upon offenders
who were mentally retarded or under age 18 at the
time of their crimes. Kennedy v. Louisiana, ___
U.S. ___, 128 S.Ct. 2641, 171 L.Ed.2d 525 (2008);
Atkins v. Virginia, 536 U.S. 304, 122 S.Ct. 2242,
153 L.Ed.2d 335 (2002); and *Roper v. Simmons*,
543 U.S. 551, 125 S.Ct. 1183, 161 L.Ed.2d 1
(2005). However, during this same era the United
States Congress enacted the death penalty for drug
kingpins who do not commit homicides, a crime
not before receiving the death penalty but admit-
tedly a statute not yet challenged before the Supreme Court. In 1999, the State of Oklahoma executed a juvenile offender who was only age 16 at
the time of his crime, the first juvenile offender
executed in Oklahoma history. Given these exam-

ples, the death penalty's "standards of decency" may be vacillating as it evolves.

§ 3.2   Pre–1970s Supreme Court Rulings

As described earlier, the death penalty has been a mainstay of American criminal law since the formation of the United States and its colonial antecedents. Its political popularity rose and fell, resulting in it being in or out of the criminal statutes, but its federal constitutionality had never been seriously questioned by defense counsel nor ruled on directly by the Supreme Court. There seemed to be a fundamental understanding that the death penalty was a fixed part of the constitutional landscape.

Some earlier cases did poke and sniff at this issue but then ultimately left it alone. For example, when the State of New York moved from hanging to the electric chair as its means of dispatching condemned prisoners, the Supreme Court was asked to examine the issue. *In re Kemmler*, 136 U.S. 436, 10 S.Ct. 930, 34 L.Ed. 519 (1890). However, in an often misinterpreted opinion, the Supreme Court in *Kemmler* held that the 8th Amendment to the United States Constitution did not apply to the states and deferred instead to the New York legislature's finding that electrocution was acceptable in their state. The Supreme Court in *Kemmler* did provide one continuing legal premise for 8th Amendment cases: "Punishments are cruel when they involve torture or a lingering death ... [S]omething more than the mere extinguishment of life."

Another important earlier case from the Supreme Court is *Powell v. State of Alabama*, 287 U.S. 45, 53 S.Ct. 55, 77 L.Ed. 158 (1932). *Powell* involved an alleged gang rape of a white girl by seven young black men near Scottsboro, AL ("the Scottsboro boys"), all of whom were convicted on questionable evidence and sentenced to death at trials essentially without defense attorneys. The Supreme Court relied upon the Due Process provision of the 14th Amendment to find a requirement for the appointment of defense counsel to represent indigent capital defendants in such cases. However, the Court limited this right to counsel to capital cases similar to *Powell*, where the capital defendants were described by the Court as "ignorant and illiterate" young black men, far away from home and facing a particularly hostile community environment. It was to be another 30 years before all capital defendants were to be guaranteed defense counsel, but in practice trial judges were fairly liberal in finding *Powell*-like situations and appointing defense counsel for capital defendants in most cases.

During the 1960s, a highly active Supreme Court under Chief Justice Warren greatly expanded the rights of criminal defendants, primarily under the 4th, 5th, and 6th Amendments to the United States Constitution. The states were required to honor these newly articulated federal rights, because they were brought under the umbrella of the 14th Amendment's requirement that states provide Due Process and Equal Protection of the Laws to criminal defendants in state courts. Also under that 14th Amendment umbrella is the 8th Amendment's prohibition of "cruel and unusual punishments." Therefore, it seemed logical to assume that the 8th

Amendment, working through the 14th Amendment, would be used either to force enormous change upon state death penalty systems or to abolish them altogether.

This almost happened in 1963, when the Supreme Court narrowly denied certiorari in *Rudolph v. Alabama*, 375 U.S. 889, 84 S.Ct. 155, 11 L.Ed.2d 119 (1963). Justice Goldberg, joined by Justices Douglas and Brennan, filed a dissent to this denial of certiorari and wanted the Supreme Court to consider whether the 8th and 14th Amendments permit the death penalty for a rapist who has not committed homicide. Goldberg wanted argument and consideration of the "evolving standards of decency" issue, as well as whether the death penalty for rape was disproportionately severe and unnecessarily cruel. However, certiorari was not granted.

As actual executions quietly ended in the mid–1960s, many social observers began to pronounce the death of the death penalty in America. However, despite aggressive litigation efforts by several anti-death penalty groups, the Supreme Court never tackled this remaining defendants' rights issue during its liberal and progressive Warren–Court era in the 1960s.

§ 3.3 Early 1970s: An End to the Old Way

By the early 1970s, Chief Justice Burger had replaced the retired Chief Justice Warren and soon was joined by several new Justices, marking a pronounced shift to a much more conservative and less active Supreme Court. Largely as a result of this timing, death penalty cases heard by the Supreme Court in the 1970s found a quite different audience. However, although the Supreme Court did not end the death penalty once and for all, the Court did terminate the system as it had existed for centuries and imposed fundamental constitutional changes upon it. The current death penalty system in the 21st century resulted from several key decisions by the Supreme Court in the 1970s, interpreting the scope of the 8th Amendment's prohibition of Cruel and Unusual Punishments as incorporated within 14th Amendment Due Process.

The Supreme Court decided *McGautha v. California* in 1971, 402 U.S. 183, 91 S.Ct. 1454, 28 L.Ed.2d 711 (1971). In one of his last opinions before retiring and being replaced by Justice Rehnquist, Justice Harlan wrote for a 6–3 majority, finding no 14th Amendment Due Process violation in permitting capital juries to have complete, unfettered discretion in choosing between the death penalty and life imprisonment. Under *McGautha*, death penalty states were free to choose to have separate hearings for the guilt stage and the sentencing stage, or they could have just one hearing, following which the jury could both convict the defendant and then impose the death sentence. *McGautha* also held that juries in capital cases need not be guided in their choice between life and death, observing that it would be nearly impossible to draft sentencing statutes to channel jury discretion in death penalty cases.

The most abrupt turnaround in the history of American death penalty law occurred just over one year later when the Supreme Court decided *Furman v. Georgia*, 408 U.S. 238, 92 S.Ct. 2726, 33 L.Ed.2d 346 (1972). Actual executions had faded completely away over five years before *Furman* was decided, and the leading anti-death penalty organizations and attorneys in the country urged the Supreme Court to hold that the imposition and carrying out of the death penalty constitute cruel and unusual punishment in violation of the 8th and 14th Amendments. However, the result in *Furman* reflects a Supreme Court still in transition from the 1960s Warren/Brennan Court to the 1970s Burger/Rehnquist Court. *Furman* includes a one-paragraph *per curiam* opinion and nine individual opinions, one by each of the Justices. Totaling 233 published pages, *Furman* is the reputedly the longest Supreme Court case opinion in history!

Furman's *per curiam* opinion is the only common ground for a five–Justice majority, and it is noteworthy for what it said and didn't say. The operative phrase is that the death penalties "in these cases" are cruel and unusual punishments, so the Court simply reversed the death sentences in the specific Georgia and Texas cases joined for consideration under *Furman*. However, despite strong urging in the concurring opinions and perhaps a good deal of wishful thinking by anti-death penalty groups, the Supreme Court in *Furman* did not hold the death penalty to be unconstitutional in all cases.

Five Justices wrote lengthy opinions concurring with the *per curiam* holding, adding their individual perspectives to that outcome. Justice Douglas reiterated the arguments from his dissent in *McGautha* the year before and stressed his fear that circa–1972 death penalty procedures leave the door open for discrimination based upon race and other inappropriate factors, in large part because they provide insufficient jury sentencing standards. Justice Brennan's opinion incorporated his concern that a punishment not be degrading to human dignity. The death penalty fails this test, according to Brennan, because it is unusually severe and degrading, it appears to be inflicted arbitrarily, society rejects the actual execution of prisoners, and the death penalty does not serve legitimate penal purposes any better than does life imprisonment.

Justice Stewart's concurring opinion in *Furman* concluded that death sentences are so "wantonly and freakishly imposed" as to be unconstitutional. Noting the several ways in which the death penalty is unique within criminal punishment, Justice White provided an often quoted description of the uniqueness of this ultimate sanction: "The penalty of death differs from all other forms of criminal punishment, not in degree but in kind." His quip as to arbitrariness has had an equal popularity since 1972: "These death sentences are cruel and unusual in the same way that being struck by lightning is cruel and unusual."

Justice Marshall's 70–page concurring opinion provided a wide-ranging discourse on the history and evolution of the death penalty, including the conceivable purposes served by it and why it could be considered to be cruel and unusual. Marshall concluded that it is morally unacceptable to the current society and is excessive and unnecessarily harsh and cruel. Rejecting the death penalty, Marshall said, permits us to join the other leading countries in the world which already have done so.

Chief Justice Burger's dissent in *Furman* reminded us that since the 8th Amendment was adopted, no Supreme Court case has ever held that the death penalty is prohibited as cruel and unusual punishment. Thus, the holding in *Furman* could be seen as an "instant evolution" in constitutional law. However, Burger's reading of the other Justices' opinions concluded that only a few would prohibit the death penalty entirely and that most find some means for it to pass constitutional muster. Given the events that were to follow *Furman*, Burger's dissenting opinion may have had its greatest impact in outlining for state legislatures the means for enacting new death penalty statutes which would be acceptable under the 8th Amendment.

Justice Blackmun's dissent in *Furman* also telegraphed future developments, in that he verifies his personal opposition to the death penalty but could not agree that it violates the 8th Amendment. Blackmun's opinion in *Furman* was written in his first year on the Court. By his last year on the Court, Blackmun had changed his mind and was to write that "*Furman*'s essential holding was correct" and "the death penalty cannot be administered in accord with our Constitution." *Callins v. Collins*, 510 U.S. 1141, 114 S.Ct. 1127, 127 L.Ed.2d 435 (1994) (Blackmun, J., dissenting).

Justice Powell, also new to the Court in 1972, added his dissent in *Furman*, finding inadequate constitutional foundation for the majority's decision. Powell was to maintain this constitutional view during his service as a member of the Court, but he stated after retirement that he was wrong and should have found the death penalty to be unconstitutional.

The final dissent in *Furman* was filed by yet another fairly new member, Justice Rehnquist. His dissent recounted the long history of the death penalty in America and castigated the Court for such a major breach of judicial self-restraint. In contrast to Blackmun and Powell, Rehnquist (later Chief Justice) did not change his views about the constitutionality of the death penalty and provided strong leadership in maintaining this view among a majority of members of the Court.

The immediate effect of *Furman* was to invalidate the Georgia and Texas death penalty statutes. However, since all of the other death penalty jurisdictions had statutes and processes with similar characteristics, the broad impact was to discontinue the imposition of the death penalty nationwide. Those offenders already sentenced to death had their sentences changed to various forms of imprisonment, and death rows became empty. Many assumed (and broadly announced) that the death penalty in America was history.

CHAPTER 4

CONSTITUTIONAL PARAMETERS OF THE CURRENT ERA DEATH PENALTY

Following the *Furman* decision, state legislatures began to amend or replace their death penalty laws rather than abandon them as many had predicted. A total of 35 of the pre-*Furman* death penalty states passed new death penalty statutes, both attempting to cure the deficiencies of the voided statutes and to remove any doubt as to state legislative support for the death penalty generally. These statutes went into effect as early as 1973, and that year marks the beginning of the current era of the American death penalty. Trial judges and juries began sentencing offenders to death for capital crimes once again, and the empty death rows began to fill up again. Within three years, 460 new death sentences had been imposed, and the American death penalty was back in business.

Media reports often refer to 1976 as the year that the death penalty was "reinstated" in the United States. However, by 1976 the American death penalty had been back up and running at full speed for several years, with hundreds of capital offenders already on death row and awaiting execution. Nonetheless, the year 1976 is significant in that a few of the earliest death sentences in this new era had made their way through trial and state appeals and now were before the Supreme Court. Therefore, 1976 is the year that the Supreme Court found the death penalty in general to be constitutional and thereby to authorize death penalty jurisdictions to proceed to actual execution of offenders already sentenced to death. Other Supreme Court decisions since 1976 have provided the final shape of the current death penalty system.

§ 4.1 Approving the Current Era Death Penalty System

The Supreme Court had its first opportunity to review these post-*Furman* death penalty statutes in 1976 when it decided several cases, the most significant of which was *Gregg v. Georgia*, 428 U.S. 153, 96 S.Ct. 2909, 49 L.Ed.2d 859 (1976). In 1973, Troy Gregg was convicted of two armed robberies and murders and was sentenced to death under Georgia's newly-amended death penalty statute. This Georgia statute was to become the model for other states seeking to enact death penalty statutes which would pass constitutional muster. It had five essential requirements for imposing the death penalty:

(1) an independent trial on guilt or innocence;

(2) a second hearing solely to determine sentence;

   (3) a finding of at least one aggravating circumstance;

   (4) an automatic review by the Georgia Supreme Court; and

   (5) comparisons to similar cases.

Continuing the internal dissonance from *Furman*, the seven members of the Supreme Court in *Gregg* who thought the death penalty was constitutional nonetheless could not agree on one majority opinion. Despite his opinion in *Furman*, Justice Stewart wrote the plurality opinion and announced the judgment of the Court in *Gregg*. Stewart's opinion spoke for seven Justices when it laid the major issue to rest: "We now hold that the punishment of death does not invariably violate the Constitution." Despite repeated attacks by a wide variety of petitioners and lawyers, the Court's fundamental ruling in *Gregg* that the death penalty is constitutional under the 8th and 14th Amendments remains the law today.

In coming to this constitutional conclusion, Stewart relied again on the "evolving standards of decency that mark the progress of a maturing society." The death penalty has a long history and precedent supporting it and was found by Stewart to be in accord with the dignity of man. A criminal punishment must avoid wanton and unnecessary infliction of pain and be proportionate to the severity of the crime, issues which will continue to be of concern but which do not prevent all applications of the death penalty. So long as they remain within these limits, legislatures are not required to choose the least severe penalty that might be effective for an offense.

In *Gregg*, the Supreme Court observed that "[t]he most marked indication of society's endorsement of the death penalty for murder is the legislative response to Furman." Here the evidence was compelling; since *Furman*, at least 35 state legislatures and the United States Congress had enacted new death penalty statutes. Another primary indicator of evolving standards for the Court is the willingness of juries in capital cases to actually sentence defendants to death. The Court was impressed that "by the end of March 1976, more than 460 persons were subject to death sentences."

Stewart's opinion in *Gregg* also explored the principle social purposes of the death penalty, thought by the Court to be retribution and general deterrence of prospective offenders. While retribution may no longer be the dominant objective, it is not forbidden. Deterrence of prospective offenders seemed to the Court to have been the subject of inconclusive research, but the Court nevertheless just "assumed" that "the death penalty undoubtedly is a significant deterrent" for carefully contemplated murders, such as murder for hire. In any event, the Court thought these issues were best addressed by legislatures.

Gregg upheld and applied the *Furman* requirement that juries in death penalty cases must be "suitably directed and limited so as to minimize the risk of wholly arbitrary and capricious action." The new Georgia death penalty statute accomplished this by requiring that the jury find at least one aggravating circumstance before it can impose death instead of life. Other checks on arbitrary and capricious death sentences are the separate trial level hearings for guilt and for sentencing and the automatic appellate review by the Georgia Supreme Court.

One final part of the *Gregg* holding that keeps reappearing in death penalty cases is the dual focus of this sentencing decision. The sentencing authority (trial jury) must give particular attention both (1) to the nature or circumstances of the crime committed, and (2) to the character and record of the individual defendant. Both the crime and the criminal must be assessed separately and individually before the life-or-death decision can be made.

Justice White's shorter concurring opinion covered most of the same issues as had Stewart's opinion. White concluded that the more detailed trial-level death penalty procedures gave him "reason to expect that Georgia's current system would escape the infirmities which invalidated its previous system under Furman," and any lingering doubts were removed by Georgia's thorough, automatic appellate review.

Justices Brennan and Marshall wrote stinging dissents but were greatly outvoted. Brennan's dissent in *Gregg* essentially mirrors his concurring opinion in *Furman*, rejecting the majority's focus on procedures and urging instead a concern for the moral issues within the essence of Due Process. Marshall followed Brennan's approach, reiterating his arguments from his *Furman* opinion, particularly as to the unnecessary excessiveness of the death penalty. Brennan and Marshall were to be true to these principles, dissenting for the remainder of their terms on the Supreme Court in every case after *Gregg* which upheld the death penalty.

With other opinions issued on the same day as *Gregg*, the Supreme Court also upheld the new Florida death penalty law. *Proffitt v. Florida*, 428 U.S. 242, 96 S.Ct. 2960, 49 L.Ed.2d 913 (1976). The plurality, concurring, and dissenting votes and opinions matched exactly those in *Gregg*, in large part because the provisions of the Florida statute were quite similar to those in the Georgia statute. The Court seemed particularly impressed by the requirement for a careful weighing of aggravating and mitigating circumstances and did not think that they were too vague and over broad to be applied in a constitutional manner.

A third death penalty decision was issued by the Supreme Court on that same day, finding the Texas death penalty process to be constitutional. *Jurek v. Texas*, 428 U.S. 262, 96 S.Ct. 2950, 49 L.Ed.2d 929 (1976). *Jurek* is of particular note both because it validated a statutory scheme fairly different from those considered in *Gregg* and *Proffitt*. Jureck also gave approval for executions to begin in Texas, which was to become the most aggressive American death penalty state in the current era. Jerry Lane

Jurek had kidnaped, raped, and killed a 10–year-old girl under heart-wrenching circumstances.

Instead of employing the more typical weighing of aggravating and mitigating circumstances, the Texas death penalty statute simply asked the jury three questions:

(1) whether the killing was deliberate;

(2) whether the offender would be a continuing violent threat to society; and

(3) whether the offender's acts were unreasonable in response to provocation by the victim.

The jury must answer "yes" to all three questions before it could impose the death penalty. The Supreme Court was convinced that Texas courts had interpreted these three questions to permit wide-ranging consideration of mitigating circumstances by the sentencing jury. By far the most significant part of the Texas statute is the prediction of future dangerousness. Although the Supreme Court recognized the difficulty of this endeavor, it was seen as akin to other criminal justice decisions such as bail and parole. Subsequent research has drawn into question the accuracy of these "future dangerousness" decisions by juries, but they remain the most critical part of the Texas death penalty statute.

§ 4.2   Rejecting Mandatory Death Penalties

Following the Supreme Court's fractured holding in *Furman*, states wishing to continue to have the death penalty went generally in one of two directions. Most read *Furman* to require death penalty statutes with clear and strong guidance for sentencing juries as they choose between life and death for convicted murderers. Prime examples of that format are the early–1970s death penalty statutes in Georgia and Florida. See *Gregg v. Georgia*, 428 U.S. 153, 96 S.Ct. 2909, 49 L.Ed.2d 859 (1976); *Proffitt v. Florida*, 428 U.S. 242, 96 S.Ct. 2960, 49 L.Ed.2d 913 (1976). However, a few other states read *Furman*, in combination with *McGautha v. California*, 402 U.S. 183, 91 S.Ct. 1454, 28 L.Ed.2d 711 (1971), to indicate that any statutory effort to control and channel jury discretion was doomed to failure. These states, such as North Carolina and Louisiana, chose instead the option of mandatory death sentencing, ostensibly removing all sentencing discretion from juries and making it impossible for bias and caprice to be a part of their sentencing decision.

As the Supreme Court was deciding *Gregg*, *Proffitt*, and *Jurek*, it also decided two cases dealing with mandatory death sentencing statutes. *Woodson v. North Carolina*, 428 U.S. 280, 96 S.Ct. 2978, 49 L.Ed.2d 944 (1976); *Roberts v. Louisiana*, 428 U.S. 325, 96 S.Ct. 3001, 49 L.Ed.2d 974 (1976). *Woodson* reviewed two of the first death sentences imposed under North Carolina's 1974 statute which made the death penalty mandatory if defendants were convicted of capital crimes. Returning again to the evolving standards of argument analysis, the Supreme Court noted that the death penalty was mandatory for several offenses when the 8th

Amendment was adopted in 1791. However, juries continually tried to find ways to avoid the harshness of this approach, often opting to refuse to convict an offender rather than see the death sentence imposed against their wishes. Instead of removing discretion from juries in death penalty cases, the mandatory death penalty had simply shifted that jury discretion from the sentencing stage to the conviction stage. By the mid–20th century, all American death penalty jurisdictions had granted sentencing discretion to juries and had abolished mandatory death penalties.

In *Woodson*, the Supreme Court held that North Carolina had departed markedly from then-contemporary standards. Mandatory death sentencing also failed to permit individualized consideration of the particular crime and offender involved and prevented meaningful appellate court review of a jury's exercise of discretion. The Louisiana case, *Roberts*, was overturned for essentially the same reasons. The Louisiana death penalty statute included a narrower group of capital crimes than did the North Carolina statute, but the fatal problems of mandatory sentencing nonetheless caused the statute to fall.

Mandatory death sentencing has not lost its appeal for some pro-death penalty advocates, and it still surfaces occasionally. For example, the Supreme Court subsequently addressed a Nevada statute that made the death penalty mandatory for a murder by a prisoner already serving life without parole. *Sumner v. Shuman*, 483 U.S. 66, 107 S.Ct. 2716, 97 L.Ed.2d 56 (1987). Reaffirming its decisions in *Woodson* and *Roberts*, the Court struck down that statute as well, in large part because it did not allow the defendant to present and argue evidence of mitigating circumstances and thus receive individualized consideration of his case.

§ 4.3   Post–1976 Major Constitutional Rulings

Although now over 30 years old, the Supreme Court's 1976 decisions remain valid and continue to control the death penalty system of the 21st century. A steady stream of death penalty rulings continued to flow from the Supreme Court for a little over a decade, but none had the sweeping impact of the 1976 cases. The post–1976 cases have served to clear up some death penalty issues mostly around the edges and focused upon narrower but important questions.

One theme from the Supreme Court has been to allow state death penalty systems to vary within the limitations set by the Court, so long as they adequately control arbitrariness. This theme began in 1976 with the approval on the same day of the Georgia statute in *Gregg* and the Texas statute in *Jurek*, despite major differences in the sentencing processes of these two states. Appellate review of death penalty cases, seemingly important in *Gregg* and *Proffitt*, came to be quite flexible under the Court's 8th Amendment analysis. For example, the Supreme Court considered the California death penalty process in *Pulley v. Harris*, 465 U.S. 37, 104 S.Ct. 871, 79 L.Ed.2d 29 (1984). While California does have review of death sentences by the California Supreme Court, that review is not required to include a proportionality analysis, comparing the sentences received for similar crimes in that same jurisdiction. The primary goal of proportionality analyses is to protect against arbitrariness and capriciousness on a statewide basis, making an effort to assure that specific kinds of crimes and offenders are treated essentially the same no matter where the case is tried. However, the Supreme Court in *Pulley* held that the California death penalty system has enough other checks on arbitrariness, so that the 8th Amendment does not require that it also provide proportionality analysis on appeal. Many states had included proportionality analysis within their death penalty statutes, but, not surprisingly, since *Pulley* those provisions of their systems have fallen into disuse.

Another perspective on the need to control arbitrariness is the Supreme Court's continuing requirement that death penalty systems genuinely narrow the class of persons eligible for the death penalty. We have limited capital crimes essentially to murder, but we know that even all murderers do not get the death penalty. The 8th and 14th Amendments require a rational process for deciding which specific murders and murderers should, after conviction, go on to be considered for the death penalty. This narrowing can be performed by the jury either at the conviction stage or at the sentencing stage, so long as it does occur. *Lowenfield v.*

Phelps, 484 U.S. 231, 108 S.Ct. 546, 98 L.Ed.2d 568 (1988).

If the defendant is found to be "eligible" for the death penalty within the narrow category, then the deliberation turns to whether or not the offender should actually be sentenced to death. In this very last stage of the trial-level process, the offender makes a plea for mercy or to be spared from the ultimate sanction because of special "mitigating" circumstances about the crime or about the offender. Some post-*Furman* statutes, such as Ohio's, were struck down because they restricted the defense too much in this effort. *Lockett v. Ohio*, 438 U.S. 586, 98 S.Ct. 2954, 57 L.Ed.2d 973 (1978). The Supreme Court in *Lockett* held that the sentencing judge or jury must not be precluded from considering in mitigation any defense evidence as to any aspect of the defendant's character or record and any circumstances of the offense. *Lockett* reminds us that even defendants who are "eligible" for the death penalty nonetheless may not receive that penalty because of additional factors about their background or about the circumstances of their crime.

The Supreme Court also has found 8th and 14th Amendment limitations on the death penalty's application to certain categories of crimes and offenders. Consistently applying the "evolving standards of decency" analysis in its death penalty rulings, the Court has drawn some broad constitutional boundaries but has avoided serious intrusions into states' freedoms to follow their own inclinations.

The most significant holding as to eligible crimes is *Coker v. Georgia*, 433 U.S. 584, 97 S.Ct. 2861, 53 L.Ed.2d 982 (1977). The defendant in *Coker* escaped from prison and committed crimes of burglary, car theft, kidnaping, and rape to further his escape. He was sentenced to death for the rape, as authorized under the Georgia death penalty statute. In this post-*Gregg* era, only Georgia had the death penalty for rape of an adult woman, although Florida authorized death for rape of a child, and juries were very reluctant to sentence rapists to death. Despite the long history of the death penalty for rape among the Southeastern states, the Supreme Court held that our "standards of decency" had evolved beyond it and held the death penalty to be unconstitutionally excessive for a rapist who does not take a life. On June 25, 2008, the Supreme Court held that the death penalty for rape of a child is unconstitutional. Kennedy v. Louisiana, ___ U.S. ___, 128 S.Ct. 2641, 71 L.Ed.2d 525 (2008). The *Kennedy* court essentially extended its Coker rationale to child rape.

Certain categories of offenders can also fall within the protections of the 8th and 14th Amendments. Juvenile offenders were one of the first to be so recognized, when the Supreme Court first held that offenders under the age of 16 could not receive the death sentence and then moved that minimum age to 18. *Thompson v. Oklahoma*, 487 U.S. 815, 108 S.Ct. 2687, 101 L.Ed.2d 702 (1988). *Roper v. Simmons*, 543 U.S. 551, 125 S.Ct. 1183, 161 L.Ed.2d 1 (2005). Both of these cases followed the evolving standards analysis. *Atkins v. Virginia*, 536 U.S. 304,

122 S.Ct. 2242, 153 L.Ed.2d 335 (2002) held that mentally retarded offenders could not be sentenced to death either.

Many other death penalty decisions have been handed down by the Supreme Court since 1976, either pruning or freeing the death penalty in a wide variety of ways. All are based on an 8th and 14th Amendment foundation, since the Supreme Court otherwise has no jurisdiction over state death penalty systems. However, the trend since the 1980s in particular has been away from imposing constitutional restrictions on the states and toward allowing death penalty states to follow individual paths. The new Roberts Court gives every indication of following this states' rights approach.

*

PART II
SUBSTANTIVE CRIMINAL LAW ISSUES

CHAPTER 5

DEFINING CAPITAL CRIMES

A capital crime is simply a crime for which the offender is eligible for capital punishment. However, the number and variations of crimes which fit this definition have fluctuated enormously over the centuries, leaving us with a fixed category but an ever-changing content within that category. This chapter provides the basic premises upon which we determine which crimes should be eligible for the death penalty and then sketches the results of those determinations over time. The category of capital crimes has both expanded and contracted as the death penalty system evolves.

§ 5.1 Basic Premises of Crime and Punishment

The fundamental characteristic that distinguishes criminal law from civil law is punishment. Those who commit crimes against society are punished by society rather than being asked to compensate the victim or other private party. These crimes range from the most insignificant jaywalking to the most horrendous mass murder. All are subject to punishment by society acting through the appropriate branch of government, but the amount of punishment varies widely from crime to crime. This range of punishments varies from very low level fines or minimal probation to life imprisonment or the death penalty. It is this latter punishment that is our concern here, but it is important to understand where the death penalty fits within the grand scheme of crime and punishment.

A simplifying factor for students of the death penalty is that we equate the perceived seriousness of a certain crime with the severity of the punishment for committing that crime. The worse the crime, the more it is punished, or at least that is our intent. Indeed, the primary way we rank crimes into felonies, misdemeanors, etc., is by the severity of the punishments authorized for committing those crimes. The death penalty is generally assumed to be our harshest, most severe punishment, so it will normally be connected to only the most serious crimes.

Before zeroing in on these ultimate crimes, the underlying structure should be understood. A basic dividing line is drawn between crimes against the person and crimes against property, with the former generally being considered to be more serious. Crimes against persons include a wide range from minor assault and battery through rape and homicide. Crimes against property include, as the label implies, either theft or destruction of things of value that belong to someone else. Such property crimes, if they involve property of great value and/or are repeated often enough by the offender, can result in very long prison sentences including life without parole. However, the general range of punishments for property crime is lower than the corresponding range of punishments for crimes against the person. Finally, property crimes cannot receive the death penalty in modern-day America, while the worst of crimes against the person obviously can and do.

Crimes against the person are generally considered to be more serious simply because the safety and security of human beings are thought to be more important and precious than even the most valuable property. The state is expected to protect people more aggressively than it protects property, and prospective offenders are expected to appreciate the greater seriousness of attacking people as compared to just stealing or destroying their property. This principle sometimes gets lost in the implementation of criminal law, particularly when the integrity of the person of some members of society is not highly respected or when the property of other members of society seems to get extraordinary protection. However, the principle remains central to criminal law in general and to death penalty law in particular.

Within this most serious general category of crimes against the person, specific crimes move from minor threats and injuries (assaults and batteries) though kidnaping and onto the most threatening crimes in American law: rape and homicide. The designated punishments increase as the injury to the victim increases, and kidnaping can be a very serious crime. Forcible rape is punished quite severely in the United States today, as it is seen as the ultimate crime against the person short of homicide.

The final category is homicide law, subdivided into an extraordinary range of crimes and corresponding punishments. All homicide crimes have the same result: the victim's life has been taken. The only variable among homicide law is the offender's criminal intent. The least serious homicide traditionally is involuntary manslaughter, essentially a reckless or grossly negligent killing, for which conviction may result in only a few years in prison. Voluntary manslaughter, despite the similar name, is a different and much more serious crime than involuntary manslaughter and is punished much more harshly. Voluntary manslaughter involves an intentional killing provoked by the victim and committed "in the heat of passion" by the offender. Long prison terms can result from convictions of voluntary manslaughter.

Murder is generally agreed to be the worst crime within the worst category of crime. Traditionally, murder was thought of as the worst crime because it was an intentional killing with malice aforethought. Taking a human life is an extraordinarily momentous act, and to do so intentionally and maliciously is thought to be a particularly terrible crime. Therefore, within the entire range of punishments available for criminal conduct, murder qualifies for the most severe punishment.

Other forms of homicide also came to be designated as murder, even though they are significantly different from an intentional, malicious killing. One covers a situation in which the offender intends only to cause serious bodily harm to the victim, but the victim's injuries result in death. Here, there is no intent to kill, but the offender is thought to be so reckless toward the victim's life that the offender should be prosecuted for murder.

Another, very common form of murder is referred to as "felony-murder." Defined in different ways by different jurisdictions, felony-murder typically covers situations in which the offender causes the death of the victim while committing another dangerous felony. For example, a rapist kills his victim during a rape of the victim, a burglar kills the resident during a burglary of a home, or a robber kills the store clerk during a robbery. Felony-murder formulations usually require only that the offender cause the death of the victim, but any further degree of specific homicidal intent may or may not be required.

Finally, within the crime of murder, this worst of all crimes, there are yet more degrees of seriousness. The most common legislative division is between first degree murder and second degree murder, although some states use other labels for these two divisions. The most well-known form of first degree murder is a murder (intentional, malicious killing) committed in a willful, deliberate, and premeditated manner. Proof of this crime usually requires evidence of clear intent to kill, a cool and deliberate manner, and some form of planning before carrying out the homicide. Other forms of intentional, malicious killings are relegated to the category of second degree murder.

Myriads of other crimes also exist but do not fit neatly into this categorical analysis. Most are business crimes, many of which can be extremely serious and damaging to a great number of victims, but we do not tend to see them in the same way as the street crimes of robbery, rape, and murder. One fairly unique crime is treason, treated as extremely serious because it threatens the very existence of a government. For this reason, treason can be punished as harshly as first degree murder.

§ 5.2 Historical Evolution of Capital Crime Category

Given these basic premises of crime and punishment, one should expect only the worst crimes to be eligible for our harshest punishment, the death penalty. This principle has remained true throughout American history, but the list of what are considered to be our "worst crimes" has varied considerably. This inconsistency comes in large part because crimes and their punishments are considered individually by legislatures. Their degrees of "seriousness" tend to be considered in the heat of headline news about the latest occurrence, and the "relative seriousness" of a specific crime in comparison to all other crimes is rarely evaluated. The politically expedient approach often is to heap punishment upon the crime of the moment, and then leave to legal scholars the dilemma of explaining why that crime is punished as it is.

Beyond this sporadic approach, a general theme over time can be discerned. In our earliest Colonial Period, we largely adopted the criminal punishment schemes of Western Europe, particularly England. During that time period, the death penalty was popular and was attached to what today would be seen as a very wide range of crimes. The Pilgrims in Massachusetts provided the death penalty for Biblical crimes such as idolatry, witchcraft, blasphemy, sodomy, and adultery, as well as to murder and manslaughter. The wholesale hanging of witches in Massachusetts in 1692 demonstrates their commitment to that approach. Most other colonies used the death penalty much more sparingly, with some Quaker colonies not authorizing it at all. Overall, by the time of our Declaration of Independence, the American colonies generally authorized the death penalty for treason, murder, rape, robbery, burglary, piracy, and sodomy. Meanwhile, in England the number of capital crimes had doubled and redoubled. By the early 19th century, England had more than 200 capital crimes, ranging from murder to the most minor theft. Two centuries later, only murder and treason remain capital offenses in the

United States, and England has completely abolished the death penalty.

The evolution of the death penalty in the southern states had different origins and took different paths. In the South, the death penalty was a primary means of keeping the slave population submissive and under control. To be sure, the death penalty was attached to the same standard crimes as in the northern colonies, as well as to major thefts, arson, statutory rape, and all forms of "crimes against nature" (buggery, sodomy, bestiality, etc.). However, in the southern slave states, the death penalty was imposed for such additional crimes as slave-stealing, inciting slave insurrection, and circulating seditious literature among slaves, all in an effort to keep people from interfering with the rights of slave owners.

Similarly, the Black Codes of the South imposed death sentences for many more crimes by blacks than by whites. In the early–19th century, Virginia law authorized the death penalty for black slaves committing any of about 70 crimes, but had only five death penalty crimes for whites. Georgia required the death penalty for a black male who raped or attempted to rape a white female, but a white male who raped a black female was punished by only a fine and/or imprisonment. The Civil War brought an official end to the Black Codes, but the same politics and attitudes persisted in southern capital punishment systems and, in a less blatant manner, throughout the country. That is, the race of the offender and of the victim continued to be important determinants of who did and did not get the death penalty.

Moving into the early 20th century, several states either abolished or greatly reduced the availability of the death penalty. The distractions of two world wars and the great depression apparently left society relatively uninterested in the pros and cons of the death penalty. The fact that society generally tended to ignore death penalty issues may have been one of the reasons that executions reached an all-time high in the 1930s. The 199 executions in 1935 are still the highest annual count in American history, followed closely by 195 executions in 1936 and 190 executions in 1938. The number of capital crimes had not particularly increased, but the willingness to impose the death penalty for existing capital crimes certainly had.

By the mid–20th century, interest in the death penalty appeared to be waning. Very few states were giving any consideration to increasing the number of crimes eligible for the death penalty, and the execution rate was falling precipitously. The death penalty seemed to be limited essentially to murder cases in the northern states, with the southern states also using the death penalty for rape. That pattern appeared to be essentially steady. In 1925, 18 states, the District of Columbia, and the federal government authorized the death penalty for rape. By 1971, that number had declined only slightly to 16 states and the federal government. A smattering of death penalty states also included treason, kidnaping, and robbery. As actual executions began to fade rapidly in the 1960s, most executions were for murder with a very few for rape or robbery.

§ 5.3 Narrowing to Murder in the Current Era

The effect of *Furman v. Georgia*, 408 U.S. 238, 92 S.Ct. 2726, 33 L.Ed.2d 346 (1972) was to knock down all death penalty statutes in the country at that time. For a short period, therefore, there were essentially no capital crimes because no constitutionally valid death penalty statutes had designated any capital crimes. However, following almost immediately on the heels of *Furman*, at least 35 states reenacted death penalty statutes and, in doing so, recreated potentially valid capital crimes in their jurisdictions. Of these 35 post-*Furman* death penalty states, 16 had authorized the death penalty for rape of an adult woman prior to *Furman* but only three (Georgia, North Carolina, and Louisiana) of those 16 reenacted that death penalty for rape. The latter two made the mistake of enacting mandatory death penalty statutes, which were struck down by the Supreme Court. *Woodson v. North Carolina*, 428 U.S. 280, 96 S.Ct. 2978, 49 L.Ed.2d 944 (1976); *Roberts v. Louisiana*, 428 U.S. 325, 96 S.Ct. 3001, 49 L.Ed.2d 974 (1976). Both states came back almost immediately with new death penalty statutes, but this time they restricted them to the crime of murder. This left Georgia all by itself in authorizing the death penalty for the crime of rape for an adult woman, although Florida and Mississippi had the death penalty for rape of a child by an adult.

Then the Supreme Court decided *Coker v. Georgia*, 433 U.S. 584, 97 S.Ct. 2861, 53 L.Ed.2d 982 (1977). Coker, serving time for murder and various other crimes, escaped from prison and broke into a nearby home, where he committed armed robbery, kidnaping, and rape. The rape conviction got him a death sentence from the Georgia jury, and the Supreme Court reviewed the case. It was very important to the Court in *Coker* that only Georgia provided for the death sentence for this crime (rape). The Supreme Court also noted that, even in Georgia, nine out of 10 cases do not result in death sentences. The Court did not discount the gravity of the crime of rape, describing it as "the ultimate violation of self" other than a homicide crime, but distinguished it from taking a human life. Therefore, the Supreme Court in *Coker* held that the death penalty for rape of an adult woman is grossly disproportionate and excessive punishment and therefore violates the 8th Amendment.

The majority opinion in *Coker* seemed to be saying that only homicide crimes could be capital crimes, but may have left the door open a tiny bit for other extremely serious crimes. Chief Justice Burger's dissent in *Coker* worried that the Court was casting doubt upon the constitutional validity of the death penalty for such crimes as treason, airplane hijacking, kidnaping, and mass terrorist activity. The *Coker* majority did not reach these possibilities, but, in the over 30 years since *Coker* was decided, murder has been the only operative capital crime across the United States.

One lingering issue from *Coker* was resolved in *Kennedy v. Louisiana*, ___ U.S. ___, 128 S.Ct. 2641, 171 L.Ed.2d 525 (2008). A narrow reading of *Coker* could limit it to rape of an adult woman and leave unresolved the question of the death penalty for rape of a child. *Kennedy* involved precisely this situation, but the Supreme Court relied upon both a national consensus against this practice and their own judgment to hold such death sentences unconstitutional. The majority opinion followed *Coker* in reiterating that, in terms of the severity of the crime and the degree of the punishment, "there is a distinction between intentional first-degree murder on the one hand and nonhomicide crimes against individual persons, even including child rape, on the other." Justice Alito's dissent agreed with the majority's premise but not their conclusion: "With respect to the question of the harm caused by the rape of child in relation to the harm caused by murder, it is certainly true that the loss of human life represents a unique harm, but that does not explain why other grievous harms are insufficient to permit a death sentence." The majority ruling in *Kennedy*, nonetheless, held that the death penalty at our current stage of evolving standards of decency is limited to "crimes that take the life of the victim." *Kennedy* expressly did not apply, however, to cases of espionage or treason.

The previously long list of crimes eligible for the death penalty over many centuries has now been reduced essentially to only homicide, but not just any homicide. Given the 8th Amendment's requirement for narrowing the class of offenders for the death penalty, in theory, at least, only the most heinous murders will qualify. Typically, throughout the United States, this "worst of the worst" crime is labeled first degree murder. This extreme narrowing of the category of capital crimes results from attempts to draw a line between the vast bulk of homicides and a small subgroup of the worst murders, with only this latter subgroup being eligible for the death penalty. In fact, over the last decade throughout the United States, only about 5% of all persons arrested for homicide have been sentenced to death and only about 1% of them have actually been executed.

This sole remaining capital crime usually can take two forms, either the traditional common law premeditated murder or some form of felony-murder (a homicide occurring during a felony such as rape or robbery). Premeditated murder theoretically assumes at least some level of planning and deliberation, so perhaps during that interim the death penalty might have a deterrent effect, again theoretically. We also tend to think that premeditated murderers are the most culpable and deserve the greatest retribution, hence the death penalty. Domestic homicide (the killing of relatives and sexual intimates) tends to be discounted in perceived seriousness and punishability, certainly as compared to homicides by and against strangers, having the effect of excluding most women's homicides as compared to men's homicides.

Felony-murder is the most common conviction for those offenders sentenced to death during the current era. The high frequency of capital felony-murder cases may be a societal statement that such forms of murder are more serious and more deserving of the harshest of punishments than instances in which persons simply kill their families without broader involvement in an additional felony. Somehow, incidentally killing the store clerk during a robbery is perceived as more heinous than stalking and planning the murder of a loved one.

Another more likely explanation is simply that felony-murder cases tend to be easier to prove. Employing the felony-murder rule makes the prosecution's job easier by not having to prove a murderous mens rea, and a jury does not have to ponder the often opaque meaning of "premeditated murder." Prosecutors, being human and anxious to prove they are "tough on crime," understandably may take this short cut to death row. However, sentencing strangers who kill the store clerk more severely than we sentence parents who murder their entire families raises serious jurisprudential questions and has a quite different impact upon male and female offenders. The question remains whether we truly are sentencing to death the "worst of the worst" of our violent criminals.

§ 5.4 Re–Expanding Capital Crime Categories

In the decades following *Coker*, we can see some effort to begin to broaden again this category of capital crimes. For example, the federal death penalty statute has been expanded to include many specific varieties of felony-murder, including causing death during a car theft, and causing death during a burglary. However, almost all of these new capital crimes are simply variations on the well-established felony-murder model. A few truly different capital crimes do exist. The crimes of espionage and treason have always been death penalty crimes in the United States, and they continue to be listed in the federal statute and even some state statutes. However, prosecution and conviction for these crimes are extremely rare, making them more symbolic than pragmatic. Another nonhomicide crime which occassionally is proposed includes being a major drug dealer. The constitutional acceptance of this is doubtful but has not been tested. Given the wide spectrum of murders receiving death sentences in the current era, from mass murder by terrorists to nearly accidental killings by amateur robbers, it seems possible that some non-homicide crimes might be considered as reprehensible as the least of these.

CHAPTER 6

AGGRAVATING AND MITIGATING CIRCUMSTANCES

Even once we have settled upon which crimes and offenders are legally eligible for the death penalty, we must then pick and choose very carefully among them in making actual selections for this ultimate sanction. In principle, we are seeking to identify not just particularly bad crimes or particularly bad criminals—we want the absolute "worst of the worst." Therefore, legislatures in death penalty jurisdictions struggle to identify the factors which will help guide the jury in making this literally life-or-death decision. Some factors, called aggravating circumstances, make the crime and the offender even worse. Other factors, called mitigating circumstances, make the crime and/or the offender seem a little less horrible or perhaps a little more understandable. The Supreme Court has developed fairly detailed tests for what can and sometimes must be included within these lists of aggravating and mitigating circumstances, so legislatures stay within these limits as they exercise otherwise fairly broad discretion in developing these statutory provisions.

§ 6.1 Requirements and Limitations

Statutes which make the death penalty mandatory for a certain crime have been held unconstitutional by the Supreme Court. *Woodson v. North Carolina*, 428 U.S. 280, 96 S.Ct. 2978, 49 L.Ed.2d 944 (1976); *Roberts v. Louisiana*, 428 U.S. 325, 96 S.Ct. 3001, 49 L.Ed.2d 974 (1976); *Summer v. Shuman*, 483 U.S. 66, 107 S.Ct. 2716, 97 L.Ed.2d 56 (1987). If everyone found guilty of a capital crime cannot automatically be sentenced to death, then the sentencing judge and jury must use guided discretion in choosing between life imprisonment and the death penalty on a case-by-case basis. This choice must take into consideration both (1) the nature and circumstances of the crime and (2) the character and background of the offender. *Gregg v. Georgia*, 428 U.S. 153, 96 S.Ct. 2909, 49 L.Ed.2d 859 (1976).

Death penalty statutes normally include a list of aggravating circumstances which would make the crime more heinous and thus the death penalty more likely. Such aggravating circumstances typically include such factors as that the crime involved more than one murder victim, the murder victim was a police officer, or the murder was committed along with another serious felony such as rape or robbery. At least one such aggravating factor must be found before the offender can be found eligible for the death penalty.

Counterbalancing these aggravating circumstances is a list of mitigating factors which make the death penalty less likely. Such mitigating factors typically include that the offender was particularly young or emotionally distressed, the offender had no previous record of serious crimes, or the murder victim somehow precipitated the crime by his behavior (*e.g.*, started the fight that resulted in his death). If the jury finds that the aggravating circumstances are equal to or outweigh the mitigating circumstances, then they are to recommend the death penalty. Usually the final sentencing decision is left to the trial judge, but the judge usually follows the recommendation of the jury. In *Ring v. Arizona*, 536 U.S. 584, 122 S.Ct. 2428, 153 L.Ed.2d 556 (2002), the Supreme Court made it clear that any aggravating circumstances upon which a death sentence is based must be found by the jury and not just by the judge. The alternative to the death penalty is life imprisonment without chance of parole.

The state is required to prove the existence of at least one aggravating circumstance concerning the specific murder committed before the defendant convicted of that murder can be sentenced to death. If that stage is reached, the defendant then tries to prove one or more mitigating circumstances in order to convince the sentencing agent (either the jury or the judge) that the death sentence should not be imposed. Thus, we have a two-step, two-stage process, first proving that the defendant has committed a terrible homicide and then deciding whether this case is one deserving of a death sentence.

This Supreme Court has held that the 8th and 14th Amendments require that an aggravating circumstance "must genuinely narrow the class of persons eligible for the death penalty." *Zant v. Stephens*, 462 U.S. 862, 103 S.Ct. 2733, 77 L.Ed.2d 235 (1983). Such narrowing can occur either at the conviction stage or at the sentencing stage, but a justification must emerge for imposing the death penalty upon one convicted murderer and not upon another convicted murderer. Again, a very small percentage of convicted murderers are sentenced to death, so why this one and not that one?

The Supreme Court also has required that any such distinguishing aggravating circumstance be sufficiently clear for it to be usable in distinguishing one murder case from another murder case in a principled manner. One particularly troublesome version of aggravating circumstances has been those seemingly with their heart in the right place, describing a particular murderer as suffering from "depravity of mind" or characterizing a particular murder as "outrageously or wantonly vile, horrible, or inhuman." See *Godfrey v. Georgia*, 446 U.S. 420, 100 S.Ct. 1759, 64 L.Ed.2d 398 (1980). If the death penalty is to be reserved for the "worst of the worst" cases, then it would seem that "depraved" murderers who commit "outrageously or wantonly vile" murders would be just the ones we want. However, the Supreme Court in *Godfrey* held that the Georgia courts had not explained in this case why Godfrey was more "depraved" than other murderers or why Godfrey's murder was more "outrageously or wantonly vile" than other murders. Arguably, all murderers are depraved and all of their murders are terribly vile, so how do we choose which ones to execute and which ones to put in prison?

Several Supreme Court cases following *Godfrey* have struggled with similar aggravating circumstances in state death penalty statutes. One was the Oklahoma statute's focus upon "especially heinous, atrocious, or cruel" murders. *Maynard v. Cartwright*, 486 U.S. 356, 108 S.Ct. 1853, 100 L.Ed.2d 372 (1988). In *Cartwright*, the Supreme Court interpreted the 8th Amendment to require that such provisions must adequately "inform juries what they must find to impose the death penalty," and the Oklahoma provision didn't pass this test. Otherwise, sentencing juries are left with the kind of open-ended discretion that was held invalid in *Furman v. Georgia*, 408 U.S. 238, 92 S.Ct. 2726, 33 L.Ed.2d 346 (1972).

The Supreme Court went the opposite way in *Arave v. Creech*, 507 U.S. 463, 113 S.Ct. 1534, 123 L.Ed.2d 188 (1993). Here, Idaho's statutory language asked whether "the defendant exhibited utter disregard for human life," seemingly also hard to use to distinguish one murderer from another. However, the Idaho Supreme Court had adopted a clear narrowing construction of this statutory provision, limiting its application to "cold-blooded, pitiless slayers." A majority of the Supreme Court held that this limiting construction was sufficiently clear to pass constitutional muster.

One final Supreme Court ruling that must be considered is *Ring v. Arizona*, 536 U.S. 584, 122

S.Ct. 2428, 153 L.Ed.2d 556 (2002). Until this ruling, five states (Arizona, Colorado, Idaho, Montana,
and Nebraska) had judge-only sentencing, so that
the findings of any aggravating factors leading to
death sentences were the responsibilities of judges
not juries. The fundamental flaw in this judge-only
death sentencing scheme was that the Supreme
Court had earlier held that a criminal defendant
has a right to a jury determination beyond a reasonable doubt of any finding of fact upon which an
increase in punishment is based. *Apprendi v. New
Jersey*, 530 U.S. 466, 120 S.Ct. 2348, 147 L.Ed.2d
435 (2000). *Ring* applied the *Apprendi* requirement
to the death sentencing process in which the specific findings of aggravating circumstances are a key
basis for imposition of the death sentence. *Ring*
holds that the 6th Amendment right to jury requires that such aggravating factors be found by a
jury and beyond a reasonable doubt.

Not only did *Ring* declare invalid the five strictly
judge-only death sentencing schemes, but it also
called into question the jury/judge hybrid procedures of Alabama, Delaware, Florida, and Indiana,
in which the jury renders an advisory verdict as to
life or death but the judge makes the ultimate
sentencing decision. In some cases, this includes the
judge sentencing the defendant to death even
though the jury has recommended a life sentence.
In the other 26 death penalty states, and in the
federal death penalty process, the finding as to
aggravating circumstances is solely a function of the
jury. *Ring* clearly approves of the processes in these

latter 26 state jurisdictions, clearly rejects the processes of the five judge-only death sentencing states, and casts constitutional doubt upon the processes of the four jury/judge hybrid death sentencing states.

The bottom line from this flurry of cases is that aggravating circumstances must suitably direct and limit the sentencing discretion of death penalty juries. Their critical role is to minimize arbitrary and capricious results in death penalty cases by carefully narrowing all murders down to death-eligible murders in a rational and logical fashion. In order to be usable by everyday juries, these narrowing factors must not be vague and ambiguous but must clearly delineate between kinds of murders. Very often, this clarity has come more from state supreme court interpretations of these statutory provisions than from the original legislative enactments. Finally, it is the trial jury, not the judge, which must find these aggravating factors beyond a reasonable doubt, at least if they are the basis of sentencing the defendant to death.

Thankfully, it has gone without saying that death penalty jurisdictions cannot use express aggravating circumstances that violate 14th Amendment Due Process and Equal Protection provisions. That is, death penalty statutes cannot require a jury to distinguish cases based upon the race or sex of the offender or the victim, particularly focusing, for example, upon black males who kill white females. While research data indicate that this latter combination of race and sex is much more likely than any other to result in a death sentence, such characteristics of crime and offender no longer are permitted to play an official role in our death penalty system as express aggravating circumstances.

The Supreme Court also has considered the appropriateness of requirements and limitations for mitigating circumstances, albeit with a much different result. Death penalty jurisdictions are generally free to list as mitigating circumstances any factors that they believe makes the crime less horrible or the offender less culpable. Only very rarely has the Supreme Court indicated that some factors must be included. One of the most obvious is the Court's observation that "the chronological age of a minor is itself a relevant mitigating factor of great weight." *Eddings v. Oklahoma*, 455 U.S. 104, 102 S.Ct. 869, 71 L.Ed.2d 1 (1982). In *Eddings*, the convicted murderer was only 16 years old at the time of his crime, and the trial judge apparently had refused to consider Eddings' youthfulness in sentencing him to death. Beyond youthfulness, the Supreme Court has noted several forms of mitigating circumstances, seemingly with approval, but has not stated so clearly that any particular one must be part of the death sentencing decision.

Probably the key difference between aggravating and mitigating circumstances in 8th Amendment law is the degree to which they are carefully limited or essentially open-ended. In striking contrast to its treatment of aggravating circumstances, the Supreme Court has held that juries must have free reign as to mitigating circumstances. *Lockett v. Ohio*, 438 U.S. 586, 98 S.Ct. 2954, 57 L.Ed.2d 973

(1978). The problem the Ohio death penalty statute had in *Lockett* was that it tightly limited the characteristics of the crime and the offender that could be considered by the sentencing judge and jury. The Supreme Court overturned that statute in an opinion written (surprisingly) by Chief Justice Burger. *Lockett* held that the 8th and 14th Amendments require that the sentencer in a death penalty case must be allowed to consider as a mitigating circumstance "any aspect of a defendant's character or record and any of the circumstances of the offense that the defendant proffers as basis for a sentence less than death."

In 2007, the Supreme Court decided three cases from Texas reiterating the *Lockett* principle. *Abdul-Kabir v. Quarterman*, ___ U.S. ___, 127 S.Ct. 1654, 167 L.Ed.2d 585 (2007); *Brewer v. Quarterman*, ___ U.S. ___, 127 S.Ct. 1706, 167 L.Ed.2d 622 (2007); and *Smith v. Texas*, ___ U.S. ___, 127 S.Ct. 1686, 167 L.Ed.2d 632 (2007). Writing for the majority in all three cases, Justice Stevens made it clear that "sentencing juries must be able to give meaningful consideration and effect to all mitigating evidence that might provide a basis for refusing to impose the death penalty on a particular individual, notwithstanding the severity of his crime or his potential to commit similar offenses in the future." *Abdul-Kabir v. Quarterman*, ___ U.S. ___, 127 S.Ct. 1654, 167 L.Ed.2d 585 (2007). In a case decided only a few months earlier, the Court had approved of comments by a trial judge that "made it clear that the jury was to take a broad view of mitigating evidence." *Ayers v. Belmontes*, 549 U.S. 7, 127 S.Ct. 469, 166 L.Ed.2d 334 (2006).

The impact of *Lockett* was to force state death penalty statutes to add to their lists of express mitigating circumstances an additional, catchall mitigating circumstance at the end. Using various wording, the statutes now allowed capital defendants to provide evidence of any listed mitigating circumstance or of any other unlisted mitigating circumstance the defendant might wish to raise. The only limitation is that these unlisted factors must be relevant either to the defendant's character or record or to the circumstances of the offense. This gives every appearance of being a blank check for defense mitigation, underwritten by the United States Constitution and enforced by the Supreme Court.

§ 6.2 Common Aggravating Circumstances

Consider some typical aggravating circumstances found in death penalty statutes. A common one is having committed a murder for hire, either as the hired killer or as the person who hired the killer to commit the homicide. A focused example of this aggravating circumstance can be found in the Arizona death penalty statute: "The defendant procured the commission of the offense by payment, or promise of payment, of anything of pecuniary value." ARIZ. REV. STAT. § 13–703(F)(4). Apparently this Arizona formulation applies only to the person doing the hiring and not to the hired killer himself. The Ohio statute is broader and much less specific:

"The offense was committed for hire." OHIO REV. CODE § 2929.04(A)(2). The Ohio formulation would apply either to the hired killer or to the person who hired him.

The inclusion of murder for hire as an aggravating circumstance in death penalty considerations is a nearly universal statement that this form of homicide is among the very worst imaginable. Interpretations of this aggravating circumstance typically apply it both to those defendants who have hired the killer and to the actual killers who have accepted payment for committing the homicides. Not only have we decided that such "contract murders" deserve maximum retribution, but we also cling to the hope that potential offenders considering such homicides might be deterred by the fact that the death penalty is more likely for them than for most other murderers. Even the Supreme Court has based its analysis upon this unproven assumption: "There are carefully contemplated murders, such as murder for hire, where the possible penalty of death may well enter into the cold calculus that precedes the decision to act." *Gregg v. Georgia*, 428 U.S. 153, 96 S.Ct. 2909, 49 L.Ed.2d 859 (1976). Such cases thankfully remain rare, but murder for hire remains a standard inclusion within lists of aggravating circumstances.

Another very common aggravating circumstance is the offender's having a previous record of violent crimes. The federal death penalty statute is particularly sweeping in this regard, including as separate individual aggravating factors (1) a previous conviction of a violent felony involving a firearm, (2) a previous conviction of an offense for which a sentence of death or life imprisonment was authorized, and (3) two or more previous convictions of violent crimes punishable by more than one year. 18 U.S.C. § 3592(C)(2), (3), & (4). If the defendant convicted of the present murder has a previous criminal record of violent crimes such as these, this makes it more likely that the defendant will receive the death penalty instead of a prison sentence for the present murder. This aggravating circumstance reflects a fundamental theme in Anglo–American criminal jurisprudence that repeat offenders should be punished more harshly than first-time offenders. Death penalty states vary as to which previous crimes should be included in this calculus, but the capital defendant's prior criminal record is always a factor.

A third common aggravating circumstance is a finding that the current homicide was part of a felony-murder. As described in § 5.3, felony-murder is the most common capital crime for which offenders are actually sentenced to death. Typically, the list of felonies which count under the felony-murder formulation is limited to only a few very dangerous felonies, such as rape, armed robbery, burglary, arson, and kidnaping. However, the federal statute sweepingly includes a death, or injury resulting in death, which occurred while committing or attempting to commit a long list of federal crimes, including destruction of aircraft or motor vehicles; violence at international airports; violence against Members of

Congress, Cabinet Officers, or Supreme Court Justices; escape or attempted escape by prisoners; destruction of property affecting interstate commerce by explosives; maritime violence; and aircraft piracy. 18 U.S.C. § 3592(C)(1).

This list of included felonies provides an extraordinarily broad net for bringing offenders into the federal death penalty system. In one sense, including the felony-murder rule as an aggravating circumstance makes the statement that the combination of a dangerous felony and an intentional homicide is particularly threatening to society and should be eligible for our most severe sanctions. In another sense, it may include a hope that the robber, rapist, or kidnaper will decide not to kill his or her victim, knowing that this added crime would increase the possible punishment from imprisonment to execution. However, this aggravating factor is so very popular with death penalty prosecutors because the elements of felony-murder are so much easier to prove than the elements of a premeditated murder not a part of another dangerous felony.

Also common is an aggravating circumstance denoting a homicide as particularly planned or premeditated. The federal statute provides a good example: "The defendant committed the offense after substantial planning and premeditation to cause the death of a person or commit an act of terrorism." 18 U.S.C. § 3592(C)(9). The California death penalty statute captures this notion by including as aggravating circumstances cases in which the defendant intentionally killed the victim "by means of lying in wait" or "by the administration of poison." CAL. PENAL CODE § 190.2(a) (15) & (19). The premise appears to be that it is worse to kill in this especially planned manner than in an intentional, but less carefully deliberated, manner. We also may hope that while the prospective murderer is lying in wait or preparing the poison, he or she might think twice about going through with the murder, knowing that the enhanced possibility of the death penalty is out there. This seems intuitively true for a planned murder, at least as compared to an impulse killing during an armed robbery, but we have no empirical research findings to verify this assumption.

Almost all death penalty statutes also include as an aggravating circumstance the murder of a police officer, prison guard, fire fighter, prosecutor, or judge committed during or because of the performance of their official duties. See, e.g., GA. CODE ANN. § 17–10–30(b)(5) & (8). Apparently such homicides are seen not only as taking the life of an innocent person but also as striking against our government's efforts to enforce our criminal laws and to protect our public safety. These aggravating circumstances also are an effort to provide some extra measure of protection for our criminal justice officials against intimidation and retaliation by homicidal criminals, but again this assumption of a deterrent effect in these cases has not been found by careful empirical research.

Finally, some death penalty statutes seem to have gotten out of hand in providing extremely long lists of aggravating circumstances. Among these, California may be leading the pack, now with more than 20 aggravating circumstances and counting. In addition to the more common aggravating circumstances outlined above, the California death penalty statute (CAL. PENAL CODE § 190.2) includes murder by using a bomb, to avoid arrest, to silence an adverse witness, by shooting from a motor vehicle, and to prevent or to retaliate against the official acts of any government official. The political reality is that legislatures are prone to reacting to news of a particularly sensational murder by making the unique mode of that murder into a new aggravating circumstance in their death penalty statute. Since almost never are any of the old aggravating circumstances removed from the statute, the list just keeps growing and growing. And, so long as the statutory language and court interpretation of an aggravating circumstance is sufficiently clear and unambiguous, the Supreme Court has permitted death penalty jurisdictions to include a wide range of factors which make a murder defendant eligible for the death penalty.

§ 6.3　Common Mitigating Circumstances

Mitigating circumstances make the death penalty less likely to be imposed. As with aggravating circumstances, they also go both to the seriousness of the crime and to the characteristics of the defendant. A very common mitigating circumstance is that the offender acted under duress or emotional disturbance at the time of the homicide. California lists as a mitigator "Whether or not the offense was committed while the defendant was under the influence of extreme mental or emotional disturbance." CAL. PENAL CODE § 190.3(d). The Ohio statute also is a typical example of the duress mitigator: "Whether it is unlikely that the offense would have been committed, but for the fact that the offender was under duress, coercion, or strong provocation." OHIO REV. CODE § 2929.04(b)(2).

Variations of this "emotional disturbance" or "duress" factor would appear to be present in many homicide cases, but finding convincing and substantial evidence of it usually is quite difficult. It seems to be at the other end of the spectrum from the aggravating circumstance of carefully planning and deliberating the murder. The social policy it codifies is that we believe emotionally disturbed and/or provoked killers to be less reprehensible than we do cold-blooded, calculating killers. If the killer is sufficiently emotional and provoked, Anglo–American criminal law traditionally reduces the killing which would otherwise be murder to voluntary manslaughter and thus completely ineligible for the death penalty. While cut from the same cloth, this mitigating circumstance assumes that the defendant's emotion and provocation were not sufficient to reduce the murder to voluntary manslaughter, but these factors, even at this lower level, should still be considered in choosing between life and death for the convicted murderer.

The list of mitigating circumstances in many death penalty statutes includes the somewhat related factor that the offender acted under the substantial domination of another. The Model Penal Code provides a typical example: "The defendant acted under duress or under the domination of another person." M.P.C. § 210.6 (4)(f). California raised the bar a little in following the Model Penal Code's lead: "Whether or not defendant acted under extreme duress or under the substantial domination of another person." CAL. PENAL CODE § 190.3(g). The presumed fact pattern is when two or more offenders were involved in the homicide, and one "forced" the other to kill the victim. Duress is not usually a defense to murder directly, but under this mitigating circumstance duress could result in convicted murderers tending to avoid the death penalty. Obviously, this mitigation goes in the direction of the weaker, dominated actor in the homicide, and the stronger, dominating actor gets no benefit from it whatsoever.

Another common mitigating circumstance goes to the defendant's mental impairment of less severity than legal insanity. For example, the Arizona death penalty statute provides for mitigation where the "defendant's capacity to appreciate the wrongfulness of his conduct or to conform his conduct to the requirements of law was significantly impaired, but not so impaired as to constitute a defense to prosecution." ARIZ. REV. STAT. § 13–703(G)(1). This form of this mitigating factor is often found in death penalty states which employ the *M'Naghten* test ("knowing right from wrong") for finding legal insanity. See § 7.4 infra. These *M'Naghten* jurisdictions then relegate this second concern for being able to conform one's conduct to the law to a mitigating circumstance at the death sentencing stage rather than an insanity defense at the earlier conviction stage. Arguably, this "impaired" capacity could come from mental illness, mental retardation, or possibly other causes. In any event, it reinforces the principle that such a convicted murderer might not deserve the maximum punishment allowed by law because his or her criminal mens rea was not and could not have been quite as sharp and intense as that of other murderers.

Despite the fact that *Roper v. Simmons*, 543 U.S. 551, 125 S.Ct. 1183, 161 L.Ed.2d 1 (2005) declared unconstitutional the death penalty for offenders under age 18, the relative youthfulness of those offenders age 18 and older who are eligible for the death penalty can still be a mitigating circumstance. *Eddings v. Oklahoma*, 455 U.S. 104, 102 S.Ct. 869, 71 L.Ed.2d 1 (1982). This is most commonly phrased in death penalty statutes in the following manner: "The youth of the defendant at the time of the crime." M.P.C. § 210.6 (4). Some statutory provisions are less clear: "The age of the defendant at the time of the crime." CAL. PENAL CODE § 190.3(i). In any event, these mitigating circumstances require that the sentencing jury consider the youthful age of a capital defendant, typically without drawing any firm age range for that consideration. Given that the peak ages for commission of homicide crimes is roughly 18 to 22, it would appear that the convicted murderer's "youth" could be raised in mitigation in most cases. There may also be some death penalty cases in which the defense has raised the particularly advanced years of an elderly capital defendant under a vague "age of the defendant" mitigating circumstance, but none have come to light.

Probably the most intriguing and debatable mitigating circumstance is the catch-all provision found at the end of the list. For example, the federal death penalty statute requires the sentencing jury to consider "[o]ther factors in the defendant's background, record, or character or any other circumstances of the offense that mitigate against imposition of the death sentence." 18 U.S.C. § 3592(a)(8). Ohio's list of mitigating circumstances ends with a more sweeping version: "Any other factors that are relevant to the issue of whether the offender should be sentenced to death." OHIO REV. CODE § 2909.04 (B)(7). This open invitation provides the defense the opportunity to present evidence as to "any other" mitigating circumstance, so long as the mitigating evidence is relevant and material to the nature and circumstances of the crime or to the character and background of the defendant. This is required, in essence, by the Supreme Court's holdings in *Eddings v. Oklahoma*, 455 U.S. 104, 102 S.Ct. 869, 71 L.Ed.2d 1 (1982) and *Lockett v. Ohio*, 438 U.S. 586, 98 S.Ct. 2954, 57 L.Ed.2d 973 (1978). The range of mitigating evidence that often comes in under such open-ended provisions includes the defendant's childhood good deeds and problems, his or her adult efforts and successes as a parent or spouse, and any remorse about the crime that the defendant may be able to display.

The ultimate goal of all of these mitigating and aggravating circumstances is to provide a complete picture of the crime and of the defendant's character and background. None of us is as angelic overall as our best good deed or as evil as our worst bad deed, and whether or not to terminate a life requires consideration and assessment of the complete range of the defendant's life. This open-ended mitigation window provides the defense with an opportunity to provide that life story for the defendant.

§ 6.4 Discriminatory Impact and Unintended Consequences

Aggravating and mitigating circumstances are intended to prevent arbitrary, capricious, and discriminatory death sentencing practices. Eighth Amendment jurisprudence underlying the employment of aggravating and mitigating circumstances to guide jury discretion assumes widespread agreement as to the factors that make a case more deserving or less deserving of a death sentence. In theory, at least, these factors should strike a universal chord, and they should not discriminate unfairly as to any particular form of homicide or as to any specific group of offenders or victims.

Of course, practice and theory don't always work in harmony. The crimes that are chosen for the death penalty, or at least singled out through aggravating circumstances, sometimes result more from media hype over a recent occurrence than an objective analysis of the comparative severity of various forms of homicide. The results can be the elevation of an impulsive shooting from a car to be the equal of the torture murder of a rape victim.

Additionally, the most common death penalty crime, felony-murder, rises to the top primarily because of ease in proving the mens rea element of the homicide. Prosecuting attorneys, sensitive to compiling an impressive won-lost record in preparation for the next political election, may be tempted to select cases for pursuing the death penalty more on ease of prosecution and likelihood of victory than on an objective analysis of severity. As a result, prosecutors lobby their state legislatures to include often expansive lists of felony-murders within the aggravating circumstances of their death penalty statutes.

Finally, crimes involving particularly "valuable victims" are more likely to receive the death penalty. Some of these "valuable victim" cases may be beyond debate, perhaps where the murder victim is a police officer or prosecutor trying to bring the offender to justice. However, other "valuable victim" cases may be less justifiable. For example, we know that murder cases with white victims are several times more likely to result in the death penalty than essentially identical cases with black victims. Although these results are well established, the causes are not fully explained. The most likely reasons reside in unconscious bias among prosecutors, judges, and jurors, when faced with the horrible death of a victim who looks like them and their family and neighbors, as compared to a victim who does not look like them and who lived in a different part of town than they do. We care much more intensely when the victims of crime or other tragedy are our friends and neighbors, rather than the unknown masses far removed from our daily life. In our views, the deaths of "our people" are more "important," the victims are more "valuable," and their murderers are more deserving of the maximum punishment.

Beyond dubious choices as to crimes, aggravating and mitigating circumstances also may discriminate in unfortunate ways in describing offenders. First, it seems apparent that most aggravating circumstances single out offenders who almost everyone would agree deserve that honor: hired murderers, repeat killers, cop-killers, and mass murderers. However, other categories of offenders may rise to the top subtly and unintentionally. For example, research data consistently indicate that male offenders of color (primarily black or Hispanic) are more commonly sentenced to death than other offenders who commit essentially the same crimes. Nothing expressly included in aggravating and mitigating circumstances pinpoints such offenders, but the results nonetheless are clear.

No body of research explains how and why race of offender is singled out, we just know that it is. A careful analysis of aggravating and mitigating circumstances might reveal that black and Hispanic offenders and their crimes are more likely to have the characteristics enumerated in aggravating circumstances and less likely to be included within mitigating circumstances. If some of those characteristics incidentally include more offenders of color than white offenders, then we would have to ask whether we are really focused on factors making the crime or the offender worse and not at least in part on race of offender.

While the over-representation of black and Hispanic murderers on death row is clear, the even more striking under-representation of women murderers is not well explained by research. What we know is that in the current era women account for about 10% of murder arrests, 2% of all death sentences imposed, and 1% of all executions. From 1900 through 2007, only 50 (0.6%) of the 8,424 total executions have been of women. This provides at least a strong appearance of sex bias in the death penalty system.

One explanation for at least a part of this apparent sex bias is that women's murders typically are not within the categories singled out for the death penalty by aggravating circumstances. For example, women who murder, as compared to men who murder, tend to kill members of their own family rather than victims of their rapes and robberies. Aggravating circumstances tend to include rape/murders and robbery/murders but not domestic murders, so women murders as a class may derive a sentencing benefit from this. It may strike many as odd that robbing a store and impulsively shooting the clerk is much more likely to get you the death penalty than methodically murdering your own infant children. Of course, women are more often the victims than the perpetrators of domestic homicide, so society's lower concern for these crimes also means that violence against women is downgraded in importance.

Other explanations for this apparent sex bias lead to the conclusion that we are simply less willing to execute women than men, no matter what the crime, and that we have permitted our aggravating and mitigating circumstances to reflect this policy. For example, research indicates that the application of the felony-murder rule has resulted in capital murder convictions for a very high percentage of men on death row but for very few women on death row. Even outside of capital cases, women convicted of murder are generally much less likely than men to have committed the homicide as part of another dangerous felony. In addition to all of the other concerns about using the felony-murder shortcut to obtain a death sentence, this aggravating factor tends greatly to punish men more than women.

Judges and juries generally find that women convicted of murder are less likely than men to have premeditated their homicides and more likely than men to have killed while impassioned, angry or in fear. More important, if the impassioned factor is in doubt, it appears that the sentencing agent is more likely to find it for women defendants than for men defendants. The research also concludes that judges and juries generally are more likely to find duress or emotional disturbance for women offenders than for men offenders in homicide cases. Even casual observance of male and female criminal defendants reveals the greater ability of women to manifest their emotions as compared to that of men, providing women's defense attorneys with more effective means of demonstrating this mitigating circumstance to a jury. The research also tells us that when a woman commits a homicide jointly with a man, judges and juries generally are more likely to find that the man was the dominant actor. This occurs with all other variables being the same and only the sex of the offender being different. If "acting under duress" is a mitigator, women are more likely to benefit from it than are men.

Finally, it is believed that judges and juries generally are more likely to find sympathetic factors in the lives and backgrounds of women than of men in homicide cases. This could be in part because female defendants may be more willing to expose this information to public scrutiny than are male defendants. This is particularly important under the "any other factors" mitigating circumstance, giving the defense attorney essentially an unimpeded opportunity to present such sympathetic factors. In combination with the other, more focused opportunities for excluding women murderers from the death penalty, this final range of mitigation may explain in part why women are such rare guests of honor in our execution chambers.

CHAPTER 7

SPECIAL DEFENSES

Even if an offender has committed the acts of a capital crime, that offender nonetheless may not be eligible for the death penalty. This possible ineligibility would result from the offender's mental state, either as diagnosed by a mental health professional or as implied from the offender's age. To be eligible for the death penalty, the criminal acts of the capital crime must be accompanied by a strong criminal intent. This mental state must be sufficiently mature, so that juvenile offenders under age 18 do not qualify. Similarly, mentally retarded offenders typically would not qualify for the death penalty because of the lower level of their mental functioning. Finally, those found to be insane after being sentenced to death cannot be executed, at least not while still insane.

§ 7.1 Insufficient Criminal Intent

As explained in chapter four, the range of crimes for which an offender can receive the death penalty has been limited essentially to a few forms of murder, with only a few other very rare capital crimes. Murder can include unlawful killings resulting only from outrageously reckless acts or incidental to the commission of a dangerous felony such as rape or robbery. However, capital murder (that eligible for the death penalty) is limited to cases in which the offender either intended to kill the victim or exhibited a reckless indifference to human life. This narrowing of the criminal intent requirement insures that the severest punishment, the death penalty, is proportionate to the crime for which it is imposed.

In *Enmund v. Florida*, 458 U.S. 782, 102 S.Ct. 3368, 73 L.Ed.2d 1140 (1982), the defendant had been the driver of the getaway car during the burglary and robbery at a farmhouse. His accomplices killed the elderly couple who confronted them unexpectedly. However, Enmund was sitting in the car by the side of the road, was not a participant in the actual killing, and had not foreseen that his accomplices would encounter anyone in the farmhouse. Under the long-standing accomplice liability rules of criminal law, Enmund was guilty of the burglary and the felony-murder of the victims as perpetrated by his accomplices. However, the Supreme Court found that Enmund personally had neither killed the victims nor had intended that the victims be killed by his accomplices. Therefore, his degree of participation in the murders was too tangential to justify the death penalty.

To be eligible for the death penalty, *Enmund* requires that the offender be convicted of a capital crime and have either killed the victim(s) himself or have an intention or purpose that their lives be taken. This minimal criminal intent for capital murder is narrower and more focused than the criminal intent for murder generally, providing yet another example of the principle that only some murderers are eligible for the death penalty.

Tison v. Arizona, 481 U.S. 137, 107 S.Ct. 1676, 95 L.Ed.2d 127 (1987), served to refine and somewhat refocus the criminal intent test from *Enmund*. The crimes involved in the *Tison* case were considerably more flamboyant and wide-ranging than those in *Enmund*. Three young men, the Tison brothers, somehow carried a large ice chest filled with guns into the prison where their father was serving time for murder. Not surprisingly, the prison escape which followed included several homicides, police shootouts, and similar events. Four victims were shot and killed by the two escaped inmates as the Tison brothers stood by and did nothing.

The *Tison* test for criminal intent clarifies and somewhat modifies the *Enmund* test. In *Tison*, the Supreme Court found that the brothers participated in the felonies in a major way and that they manifested a "reckless indifference to human life" as they did so. Surely providing guns to dangerous inmates and joining them in an armed escape from prison easily falls within those requirements. The Tison brothers probably were eligible for the death penalty under the original *Enmund* test, and the Supreme Court removed any doubt with the more refined *Tison* test. After *Tison*, prosecutors in capital murder cases must prove that the defendant was a major participant in the murder and had a reckless indifference to human life. Any lesser level of

criminal intent renders the death penalty disproportionately severe in comparison to the crime.

§ 7.2   Below Minimum Age

Even if defendants have committed capital murder and qualify for the death penalty under *Enmund* and *Tison*, they may be too young to be
sentenced to death. The 8th Amendment to the
United States Constitution now requires a minimum age of 18 at the time of the crime, and the
majority of death penalty states already had minimum ages of 17 or 18 directly in their death penalty
statutes.

In addition to this minimum age floor for the
death penalty, even those capital defendants a few
years older than the minimum may have the right
to consideration of their youthfulness by the sentencing judge and jury. *Eddings v. Oklahoma*, 455
U.S. 104, 102 S.Ct. 869, 71 L.Ed.2d 1 (1982), in
considering the death penalty for a 16–year-old offender, established that, at a minimum, "the chronological age of a minor is itself a relevant mitigating factor of great weight." This mitigating factor
was reaffirmed in *Roper v. Simmons*, 543 U.S. 551,
125 S.Ct. 1183, 161 L.Ed.2d 1 (2005). Children
generally do not have adult rights and responsibilities in any area of the law, and death penalty law is
no exception.

Seven years later in *Thompson v. Oklahoma*, 487
U.S. 815, 108 S.Ct. 2687, 101 L.Ed.2d 702 (1988),
the Supreme Court held that executions of offend-

ers under age 16 at the time of their crimes are prohibited by the 8th Amendment to the United States Constitution. Wayne Thompson was only age 15 when he was involved in a capital murder. The combined effect of the four-Justice plurality opinion by Justice Stevens and the concurring opinion by Justice O'Connor in *Thompson* was to hold that no state without a minimum age in their death penalty statute can go below age 16 without violating the Constitution, and in fact no state with a minimum age in its death penalty statute was using an age of less than 16.

One year later, the Supreme Court decided *Stanford v. Kentucky*, 492 U.S. 361, 109 S.Ct. 2969, 106 L.Ed.2d 306 (1989), examining the combined cases of a 16–year-old offender and a 17–year-old offender. *Stanford* left the minimum age at 16, declining to find a federal constitutional mandate placing that minimum age at 17 or 18. Again it took the combined effect of Justice Scalia's four-Justice plurality opinion and Justice O'Connor's concurring opinion to reach this holding. Highly sensitive to states' rights to determine their own death penalty policies and procedures, the Supreme Court in *Stanford* declined to find a national consensus establishing the minimum age at 18.

Quite aside from the mandates of the 8th Amendment to the United States Constitution, state constitutions are also a source of regulation for the juvenile death penalty. In *Brennan v. State*, 754 So.2d 1 (Fla.1999), the Florida Supreme Court interpreted the Florida Constitution as barring the execution of Keith Brennan because he was only 16 years old at the time of his crime. Noting they were not bound by the rulings of *Thompson* and *Stanford* in interpreting the requirements of the Florida Constitution, the Florida Court nonetheless did follow much of the same analytical approach. While the Florida Supreme Court paid due deference to the United States Supreme Court's interpretation of the United States Constitution, the ultimate interpreter of the Florida Constitution is, of course, the Florida Supreme Court.

The most recent and apparently final Supreme Court case on this issue is *Roper v. Simmons*, 543 U.S. 551, 125 S.Ct. 1183, 161 L.Ed.2d 1 (2005). Christopher Simmons was 17 years old when he committed murder in Missouri, and the Supreme Court reversed *Stanford* to hold that the minimum age for the imposition of the death penalty is age 18. In the time between 1989 and 2005, the Court held (5–4) that the "evolving standards of decency" had brought us to the point that the death penalty for 16– and 17–year-olds was no longer acceptable under the 8th Amendment to the United States Constitution. More states were prohibiting it, fewer juries were imposing it, and no other country in the world condoned it. In addition, the Court's 2002 decision in *Atkins* had found the death penalty for mentally retarded defendants to be unconstitutional for reasons that apply with equal or greater force to juveniles. *Simmons* removed 72 juvenile offenders who were on the death rows of 12 states and ended our three and a half centuries of executing juvenile offenders.

All of these cases were decided by the narrowest of margins: *Eddings* was a 5–4 decision, *Thompson* was a 4–1–3 decision, *Stanford* was a 4–1–4 decision, and *Simmons* was a 5–4 decision. Nonetheless, state courts have uniformly recognized and enforced these Supreme Court holdings without questioning their validity or staying power. The constitutionality of the death penalty for juvenile offenders appears to be settled, at least so far as making youthfulness a mitigating factor of "great weight" and prohibiting executions for crimes committed below age 18.

§ 7.3　Mentally Retarded

A first cousin to the juvenile death penalty issue is the concern about the death penalty for mentally retarded offenders. One overly simplistic characterization of mental retardation is that it is comparable to having the mental age of a 10–year-old or a 14–year-old. If so, then opponents argue that the mental age should determine death penalty eligibility, and mentally retarded offenders should be excluded just as juvenile offenders under age 16 or 18 are excluded.

When the issue first arose before the Supreme Court, it refused to hold that the death penalty for mentally retarded offenders is cruel and unusual under the United States Constitution. *Penry v. Lynaugh*, 492 U.S. 302, 109 S.Ct. 2934, 106 L.Ed.2d

256 (1989). John Paul Penry had an IQ of 50 and the mental age of six, never having finished the 1st grade. In *Penry*, the Supreme Court found no constitutional bar to the death penalty for mentally retarded capital defendants, primarily because at that time (1989) only two death penalty jurisdictions expressly prohibited it. Two states did not constitute a national consensus under the Supreme Court's "evolving standards of decency" analysis.

However, the issue did not fade away after 1989. An intensive political action campaign kept the death penalty for the mentally retarded in the news media, and state legislatures in death penalty states were asked to address the issue. As a result, nearly half of the death penalty jurisdictions amended their death penalty statutes in the 1990s to exclude mentally retarded offenders, generally using an IQ cutoff of below 70, and this legislative movement continued to grow steadily in the early years of the 21st century.

The Supreme Court's June 2002 decision moved 8th Amendment law on this issue. *Atkins v. Virginia*, 536 U.S. 304, 122 S.Ct. 2242, 153 L.Ed.2d 335 (2002). Daryl Atkins and an accomplice had committed a robbery-murder, but Atkins had an IQ of 59 and the mental age of a nine- to twelve-year-old child. Concluding that the flurry of legislative activity, in conjunction with other indicators, established a national consensus opposing the death penalty for the mentally retarded, the Supreme Court in *Atkins* held that this application of capital punishment is cruel and unusual under the 8th and 14th Amendments. In addition to being rejected by a growing number of state legislatures, the actual imposition of death sentences and actual executions upon mentally retarded offenders is quite rare even in states which permit it, providing yet further indication of a national consensus against it. One lesser issue involved the opposition to this practice found in public polls, in the positions of leading organizations, and in comparative and international law. The majority in *Atkins* relied in small part on these findings, but the three dissenting Justices thought that a "national consensus" in constitutional law should not be built upon the whims of public opinion or upon the practices of other countries.

In establishing this national consensus under the evolving standards of decency, the Court in *Atkins* also measured it against the social purposes served by the death penalty: retribution and deterrence of capital crimes by prospective offenders. The Court held that mentally retarded offenders have less culpability for their crimes and therefore do not merit maximum retribution. The Court in *Atkins* also evaluated potential offenders' ability to deliberate and premeditate their murders, finding "that sort of calculus is at the opposite end of the spectrum from behavior of mentally retarded offenders." Given this basic truth, they were unlikely to be deterred from murderous conduct.

While *Atkins* held that the 8th and 14th Amendments prohibit execution of the mentally retarded, the Supreme Court left to the States the task of developing ways to define this category. This smacks of a macabre game of "you can't execute them but we won't tell you who they are," but it is the same approach used by the Court in regard to executing the insane. Following *Atkins*, we have seen a flurry of state legislative activity to amend death penalty statutes, both to prohibit the execution of the entire category of mentally retarded offenders and to define who is and is not in that category. The several hundred apparently mentally retarded inmates on death row at the time *Atkins* was decided also are litigating their cases one by one to see if they fall within the protection of *Atkins*.

§ 7.4 Legal Insanity

Assuming that a capital defendant has the requisite strong criminal intent, is at or above the minimum age, and is not mentally retarded, one last "state-of-mind" defense exists. Often lumped together under "legal insanity," these defenses apply to all criminal cases but may have particular significance in death penalty cases. Capital murders often are so horrendous that one immediately assumes that the perpetrator must be mentally ill. Most probably are, but the family of insanity defenses focuses not on the defendant's psychiatric illnesses but instead on the appropriateness and fairness of subjecting the defendant to a criminal trial and to criminal punishment.

Variations on this issue arise at three primary stages. First, in order for a capital defendant (or any criminal defendant) to stand trial, the defendant must be mentally competent. In *Dusky v. United States*, 362 U.S. 402, 80 S.Ct. 788, 4 L.Ed.2d 824 (1960), this was characterized as a reasonable ability to consult with the defense lawyer and a rational and factual understanding of the criminal proceedings.

The second variation, also not unique to death penalty cases, is the issue of the defendant's legal sanity at the time of the crime. The most common insanity test, simply knowing right from wrong, comes from England's *M'Naghten's Case*, 8 Eng. Rep. 718 (H.L.1843). The *M'Naghten* test has evolved under modern statutes in this country to become whether the defendant, as a result of a severe mental disease or defect, was unable to appreciate the nature and quality or the wrongfulness of his acts. Other jurisdictions have adopted an insanity test that includes not appreciating the wrongfulness of one's acts but adds the alternative of not being able to conform one's conduct to the requirements of the law. Being found legally insane at the time of the crime typically avoids the being actually convicted of the crime, but instead defendant is committed to a mental institution or sometimes to a prison to receive treatment. Since they cannot legally be punished, they obviously cannot receive the death penalty.

The final variation is the onset of insanity only after being convicted and sentenced to death. Given stays on death row awaiting execution of 10 to 20 years and longer, it seems unsurprising that some death row inmates might go off the deep end mentally. The Supreme Court in *Ford v. Wainwright*, 477 U.S. 399, 106 S.Ct. 2595, 91 L.Ed.2d 335 (1986), has held that a presently insane death row prisoner cannot legally be executed. This is well-established in common law and in the laws of all death penalty states. The Court in *Ford* held that the imposition of the harshest form of retribution upon the insane was unjustified and offensive to civilized humanity. However, as with not executing the mentally retarded, the *Ford* prohibition as to the legally insane did not define "legal insanity" at this stage of the process. It presumably is different from competency to be tried and sanity at time of the crime, but the Court provided little guidance beyond the questions of whether the prisoner is aware of the punishment about to be imposed and why it is being imposed. Even if the prisoner has identified the link between his crime and the pending execution, this may not be enough. A prisoner's "gross delusions stemming from a severe mental disorder may put an awareness of a link between a crime and its punishment in a context so far removed from reality that the punishment can serve no proper purpose." *Panetti v. Quarterman*, ___ U.S. ___, 127 S.Ct. 2842, 168 L.Ed.2d 662 (2007) This area of law is still developing, but *Panetti* has opened the door to cases of delusional understanding that may appear to be rational.

An even more difficult problem considered in *Ford* comes in devising an acceptable procedure for dealing with death row prisoners who claim that they have become insane. In order to clear the death row inmate for execution, a fair and objective process must consider the inmate's claims, have the inmate examined by a mental health professional, and make a careful and rational decision. Of course, even if the inmate is found to be presently sane after such a careful process, the inmate might claim to have slipped into insanity since being examined, and the cycle could start all over again.

Two states have tried to solve this problem by imposing medication upon an insane death row inmate in order to make him sufficiently sane for at least a short time so that they could execute him. In *State v. Perry*, 610 So.2d 746 (La.1992), the Louisiana Supreme Court held that the state could not forcibly medicate a prisoner in preparation for execution. The Pennsylvania Supreme Court held just the opposite, allowing forcible medication. *Commonwealth v. Sam*, 952 A.2d 565 (Pa.2008). Of course, a state could earnestly try to cure a death row inmate's insanity through aggressive, long-term treatment, but the end result would be execution, a macabre example of "the operation was a success but the patient died." Various medical, psychiatric, and psychological associations have declared it unethical for mental health professionals to treat death row prisoners in preparation for their execution.

One unique issue regarding the mentally ill offenders and the death penalty is just beginning to emerge. It posits that some mentally ill capital defendants who are not legally insane (and thus can be tried and convicted of capital crimes) should nonetheless not be eligible for the death penalty.

The Supreme Court in *Atkins* and *Simmons* identified mental and emotional characteristics that render mentally retarded or juvenile capital defendants less culpable for their crimes and less able to understand and participate in their trials. This issue asks whether some mentally ill capital defendants have very similar mental and emotional characteristics and therefore should be excluded from the death penalty as are juveniles and the mentally retarded. This issue is just beginning to make its way into state legislative considerations and is very far from success.

PART III
TRIAL–LEVEL
PROCEDURAL ISSUES

CHAPTER 8

OVERVIEW OF ARREST
THROUGH EXECUTION

Before immersing ourselves in a blow-by-blow description of trial procedures in death penalty cases, consider an overview of the entire process, beginning to end. A significant characteristic of this process is that it bounces back and forth between a series of only slightly-connected agents and agencies, resulting in a process with striking inconsistencies and problems. One is tempted to refer to our death penalty system as a real-world comedy of errors, but then comes the reminder that it is this system and process that determines literally whether the subject lives or dies. In this jumbled arena, it may be particularly helpful to keep one eye on the overall process from beginning to end as we dissect each stage of that process. Only a few parts of the death penalty process are unique to capital cases, with by far the majority simply following routine

111

felony procedures in the local jurisdiction. However, it is important to comprehend the entire process from investigating the crime to executing the offender, including the routine with the exotic.

§ 8.1   Police and Prosecutor Stages

To begin at the beginning, the death penalty process is precipitated by the commission of a capital crime. As described in chapter 5, a capital crime is almost always murder. However, more than 16,000 murders occur each year throughout the United States and well under 160 (1%) of them will result in death sentences for the offenders. Therefore, when a murder occurs, the initial police investigation begins the same but with little chance statistically of generating a case that results in a death penalty.

As compared to often unreported crimes such as theft and sexual assault, homicide crimes usually become known to the police. Dead bodies are hard to ignore, and it is not left to the victim whether or not to report the crime. As a result, we can assume that the police investigate, at least to some degree, perhaps 95% of all homicides. A few probably escape police attention, particularly those cases in which people simply disappear and no one knows where they went or what happened to them. Undoubtedly some of these "missing person" cases are actually criminal homicides, but the police never develop sufficient evidence to place them in that category.

Assume we have a dead body, and death seems likely to have been by other than natural causes. The police are notified, descend upon the scene, and begin to gather physical evidence and statements from witnesses and possible suspects. At this point, the investigative process is quite dynamic and fluid, with seldom any clear indication that the case might become a death penalty case. The crime scene is totally controlled by the police, with no prosecutors, defense attorneys, or criminal court judges around to give guidance or advice. Nonetheless, the evidence and statements gathered even at these earliest stages tend to become key issues of contention at subsequent hearings, trials, and appeals.

Of these roughly 16,000 murders annually, only about 10,000 (about 62%) result in arrest of the probable offender(s). This means that in more than a third of all murder cases, we never catch the murderer and therefore never impose any sentence at all upon him or her. In large cities, nearly half of the murders do not result in any arrests. Consider the impact of this fact on our political rhetoric that murderers will be punished severely, perhaps even by the death penalty. In fact, a very large proportion of murderers receive no punishment at all because they are never caught by the police.

But let's stick with that roughly two-thirds of murder cases which do result in the arrest of one or more apparent offenders. Usually the investigation of this crime and the possible culprit(s) is conducted exclusively by the local law enforcement agency, typically the city police. Homicide cases tend to make the news, so the police (and the police chief and the mayor) often are investigating these cases under considerable media pressure to "solve" the crime and to "catch the bad guy" as quickly as possible. Research on the more than 125 innocent persons recently released from death rows indicates that this intense pressure on the police can and does cause them both to make mistakes from hurrying the investigation and to settle upon one possible suspect too quickly, ignoring persuasive evidence pointing to other suspects. Once having arrested that suspect, it is understandably difficult for the police to admit error, release the arrestee, and begin again the investigation of the crime.

If the homicide crime being investigated is truly extraordinary (multiple victims, terrorist bombing, etc.), the police may call in someone from the prosecutor's office early in the investigation. However, in the vast percentage of murder cases, the police simply complete their investigation, arrest the apparent murderer, and then turn the case over to the prosecuting attorney. This transfer of control over the case is very important. The law enforcement agents are most often city police, or perhaps county sheriffs or state police, working for those specific governmental units. The lawyers in the office of the prosecuting attorney (called district attorney or parish attorney in some states) almost always will be working for an elected county prosecuting attorney. Elected prosecutors are not beholden to anyone other than the voters who elected them. While prosecutors and the various law enforcement agencies all work for the executive branch of the government, they often are strongly divided between city, county, and state levels and not always as cooperative as might be desired.

Now the case is on the prosecutor's desk with the police investigation essentially completed, the alleged perpetrator locked up in the local jail, and the local media continuing to make this their lead story every day. Whether or not the arrested person is charged with any crime, let alone a capital crime, is solely within the discretion of the prosecutor. In some cases prosecutors are required to work through grand juries, but modern procedures give prosecutors almost complete control over the actions and decisions of grand juries. The prosecuting attorney analyzes the evidence gathered by the police, talks with the investigating police officers, and decides whether or not the case can be proven beyond a reasonable doubt before a trial jury. In addition to the guilt issue, the prosecutor also thinks about the sentencing stage. This is a major juncture for murder cases, sending most along the noncapital route but selecting some for pursuing the death penalty. This prosecutive discretion is exercised in almost all jurisdictions with no oversight, no review by any higher authority, and no involvement by the defense attorney. It is fairly common, however, for the prosecutor to confer with members of the victim's family to see what punishment they would prefer for the defendant.

An interesting exception to the typical state process is the federal death penalty charging procedure. A fairly elaborate process is followed in the local United States Attorney's office to determine if they want to go for the death penalty. If the answer is yes, then that local United States Attorney must take the request to the office of the United States Attorney General in Washington, D.C., where it is considered and debated even more. In the end, the Attorney General of the United States must personally authorize any and all death penalty prosecutions under the federal death penalty statute. Of course, federal death penalty cases constitute about 1% of all death penalty cases nationwide, so the federal process may have more symbolic importance than practical impact.

If the prosecutor's office decides to charge the arrestee with a capital crime, the next step is for the prosecutor to formally charge the arrestee (now the defendant), either through a grand jury indictment or by filing an "Information" with the local criminal court. Typically at this point of the process, the police investigation is completely wrapped up, the prosecutor has independently investigated the case, and the "state" is essentially ready to go to trial. The focus of the crime has moved from an investigation to a criminal case, with an assigned docket number and a name: *e.g., State of Wherever v. John Doe*.

§ 8.2   Trial Court Stages

Even after *State v. Doe* is officially a case, about a year may pass before it comes to trial. Early in this lengthy pretrial process, one or two defense attorneys will be appointed to represent the capital defendant. In rare capital cases, the suspect/arrestee/defendant has retained criminal defense attorney from the beginning of the crime investigation, but a very high percentage of these cases involve defendants who do not have the means to pay for their own attorney. These defendants have counsel appointed to represent them, either from a public defender's office or from the private bar. Such counsel typically are appointed soon after the prosecutor has filed the official charges.

Defense counsel typically comes into the case without any prior knowledge of it and begins to study the case and consider defense strategies. Remember that the prosecutors have completed their investigation and are essentially ready to go to trial at this point, while the defense attorney is still back at square one. Many have noted that the defense attorney plays a game of ''catch-up'' from there on. It is very common today for defense teams to include investigators and mitigation specialists as well as criminal lawyers, all working together to prepare the case both for the guilt stage and for the sentencing stage. Defense investigation of the case begins with a series of interviews with the jailed defendant and then starts to cover much the same ground already covered by the police and the prosecutor.

In the typical capital case, the year or so between charging the defendant and actually getting to trial is filled with a plethora of defense motions challenging the admissibility of the evidence gathered by the state, the potential bias of a jury picked from the local community, the constitutionality of key provisions of the state's death penalty statute, and anything else the defense team can think of to throw into the pot. This prolonged pretrial skirmishing often shapes the case in ways important to the lawyers on both sides, telling them what police-gathered evidence will be admissible at trial, what the witnesses' testimony can be expected to establish, and what specific defenses will be pursued.

Another important theme in these early pretrial stages is the possibility of a "plea bargain," a negotiated arrangement under which the capital defendant pleads guilty either to a noncapital crime or to the specified crime but without the death penalty. Negotiated pleas are an essential lubricant for the entire criminal justice system, with approximately 90% of all criminal cases resolved in this manner. The Supreme Court has recognized negotiated pleas as sufficiently voluntary to satisfy Due Process concerns. See *Brady v. United States*, 397 U.S. 742, 90 S.Ct. 1463, 25 L.Ed.2d 747 (1970). Such guilty pleas allow the state to avoid very costly and lengthy death penalty trials and still to gain a conviction and (typically) very long prison sentence for a murder defendant. The capital defendant, obviously, avoids a sentence of death, even though their "first choice" is to spend the rest of his life in prison.

Brady recognizes that the pure "voluntariness" of such pleas is always tainted somewhat by promises of a more lenient sentence, but that is to be expected and does not render them unconstitutional. However, this "taint" is especially strong in death penalty cases. In some jurisdictions, it appears that prosecutors are using their discretion to charge fairly routine murder cases as death penalty cases, primarily as a tactic to induce guilty pleas in return for "only" life sentences. Regardless of the statistical unlikelihood of a death sentence actually being imposed, capital defendants and their attorneys are reluctant to take a chance. Unfortunately, the Supreme Court recently declined a case exploring this issue. *Arave v. Hoffman*, ___ U.S. ___, 128 S.Ct. 749, 169 L.Ed.2d 580 (2008).

Assuming the capital case makes it past these various detours, it will be scheduled for trial. The first key step is to select the trial jury which will decide both the guilt of the defendant and, if convicted, whether to sentence the defendant to death. This jury selection process, explained in more detail in chapter 9, is quite complex and lengthy. Very often, just picking a capital jury can take days or even weeks, with the trial judge and attorneys plowing through an extensive list of prospective jurors. The goal is to weed out not only those prospective jurors who may be biased about this particular case or who could not sit through an intense and lengthy trial, but also those whose general feelings about the death penalty (either pro or con) would prevent them from being able to make a reasoned decision in an actual death penalty case. Once we have settled upon a jury of 12, along with a few alternates, the trial is ready to begin.

The trial of a capital crime involves two distinct stages, the first dealing with the defendant's guilt and the second focused solely upon the sentence to be imposed. The hearing at the guilt stage is nearly identical to a routine felony trial not involving the death penalty, the appearance and procedures of which have been made familiar by television and movie portrayals over many years. Prosecuting and defense attorneys make opening and closing statements to the jury, sandwiched around a parade of physical evidence and witness testimony. Following this presentation of evidence, the jury is instructed by the trial judge as to the applicable law to be applied in the case. The jury then retires to the jury room to decide, beyond a reasonable doubt, whether the defendant is guilty of the crime(s) as charged. If not convicted of a capital crime, the jury is discharged and the judge takes care of any remaining duties. However, if the defendant is convicted of at least one capital crime, the jury remains empaneled to perform its duties in the sentencing stage, which commences immediately following the jury's guilty verdict.

The sole question before the trial jury at the sentencing stage is whether this now-convicted murderer should be sentenced to death or to some form of long term imprisonment. Here, the opening and closing statements of the prosecution and defense are sandwiched around evidence as to aggravating and mitigating circumstances (see chapter 6). This same jury has just concluded beyond a reasonable doubt that the defendant committed a terrible murder, so they can be assumed to begin this consideration with a very bad "first impression" of the defendant. Therefore, the defense presents mitigating evidence in an effort to sketch out the defendant's life other than the incidence of the terrible crime. Once all of that evidence is submitted to the jury, they retire once again, this time to decide the life-or-death fate of the defendant. When they reassemble one last time in the trial courtroom, it is to inform the court (and the defendant) of the sentence which is to be imposed. Now typically exhausted, the jury finally is dismissed to return to their normal lives, and the defendant moves on either to a life in prison or the uncertainty of death row and possible execution.

§ 8.3 Appellate Court Stages

Every felony conviction and resulting sentence can pursue an elaborate and very lengthy process of challenges to that conviction and sentence, but relatively few prisoners really exhaust the possibilities. It is typically the death row inmate (and his or her lawyers) who can be expected to wring every last drop out of this process. It has two primary divisions, the first being direct appeal of the trial-level conviction and sentence and the second being post-conviction or habeas corpus challenges following direct appeals which were unsuccessful. When this process is followed aggressively, at least half to two-thirds of death penalty cases are reversed.

Our case of *State v. Doe* will first be appealed to a state appellate court. In many states, that would be an intermediate state court of appeals, but in some states it would be the state supreme court. A couple of very active death penalty states, Oklahoma and Texas, have specialized courts of criminal appeals that handle nothing but criminal cases, freeing their other state appellate courts to handle the crush of other appellate business. No matter which state court it lands in, *State v. Doe* will be briefed thoroughly by the appellant-defendant, raising every reasonable fundamental legal challenge and exposing every perceived error made at trial. Then the respondent-state will file its brief, refuting the appellant's claims and assertions. Often the parties also make oral arguments before the court, and then the court tries to decide the case. Given the caseload of many state appellate courts, decisions in these cases can be many months or even years in coming. Meanwhile, the condemned prisoner sits on death row in the state's maximum security prison.

If the petitioner is unsuccessful at the intermediate state appellate court, then typically the case can be appealed to the state supreme court. In many jurisdictions, the state supreme court does not have to hear the case but may do so if it wishes. Given the major importance of death penalty cases in most jurisdictions, they do tend to get picked for discretionary review, certainly more often than other cases. Pretty much the same routine will be followed as in the first appellate review, with briefs being filed and oral argument being made by the respective attorneys. The state supreme court then spends as much time as it needs to decide the case, ranging from months to years in some instances. Assuming the state supreme court denies relief to the petitioner, the case can be taken directly to the United States Supreme Court, but the chances of the Supreme Court agreeing to hear the case at this juncture are less than 1%.

The direct appeals process now being over, the death row inmate can and almost always will begin the state collateral attack process. If the appeals are seen as a continuation of the original criminal proceeding (*State v. Doe*), the collateral attack or habeas corpus proceedings are seen as a civil lawsuit challenging the legality of the prisoner's criminal conviction and sentence. It typically will be labeled as the petitioner versus the prison warden or state director of corrections (*John Doe v. Sarah Smith, State Director of Corrections*). The first step in *Doe v. Smith* is for the petitioner-defendant to file the case in a state trial-level court, typically in the county in which the death row inmate is now being imprisoned. Unlike the appellate courts, habeas courts are not limited to issues raised at trial but typically may undertake independent fact-finding if warranted. Although this is a trial level court, these collateral challenges are presented solely to the judge with no jury involved in any way.

If the death-sentenced petitioner loses at this state collateral proceeding, then the case begins to work its way back through the state appellate process, this time as a collateral attack (*John Doe v. Sarah Smith*) instead of as a criminal appeal (*State of Wherever v. John Doe*). The state appellate courts may be asked to rule on some of essentially the same issues they considered in *State v. Doe* during the previous appellate process, but *Doe v. Smith* in the collateral process also will raise issues which were not a part of the appellate case. In any event, the case typically will be considered by an intermediate state appellate court, and/or a specialized state court of criminal appeals, and/or the state supreme court. The same process of written briefs and oral arguments applies, and the case can take years to make its way through the various levels of state collateral attack. As before, the final step would be to ask the United States Supreme Court to hear the case, but again this has about a 1% chance of happening.

If the death row inmate has lost at trial, lost through the direct appeals process, and lost through state collateral attack, then he or she will turn to the federal habeas corpus process. The federal process cannot start until all of the state processes have been completed. This is a new, federal lawsuit, although often raising almost all of the same issues raised in the state collateral attack proceeding. It is filed originally in a federal district (trial-level) court located in the same geographical area as the state's death row prison. In essence, such cases assert that a state is depriving the petitioner of the rights to "life, liberty, and property" that are guaranteed by the United States Constitution and other federal laws. Thus, a federal district court reviews the state proceedings and may have a fact-finding hearing if deemed necessary. After presenting the case to this federal judge, the death row inmate, the defense attorneys, and the state's attorneys wait for a ruling by the federal district judge.

Assuming the petitioner-defendant loses in the federal habeas corpus action at the district court level, he or she can be expected to appeal that decision to the federal circuit court of appeals for that geographical circuit. Again, written briefs are filed and oral arguments are made, and then the circuit court retires to decide the case, sometime in the months or years to come. If the death row inmate loses at this level, he or she has one more opportunity to petition the United States Supreme Court to agree to hear the case. While the chances of the Supreme Court hearing the case at this juncture may be slightly greater than before, the probability is still very slight.

Now, typically at least eight to ten years after being sentenced to death, the condemned murderer has exhausted the obvious court challenges. To be sure, his or her attorneys can be expected to continue to seek court relief in a variety of other peripheral challenges, but the major line of appellate and collateral attack cases are over and almost always cannot be revived. Even if new evidence is discovered strongly suggesting that the death row inmate is in fact innocent and wrongly convicted, these court processes are rarely available to grant relief. *Herrera v. Collins*, 506 U.S. 390, 113 S.Ct. 853, 122 L.Ed.2d 203 (1993); *House v. Bell*, 547 U.S. 518, 126 S.Ct. 2064, 165 L.Ed.2d 1 (2006).

§ 8.4   Clemency and Execution

If John Doe's death sentence is among that minority of death cases not reversed by the courts, then his final effort to avoid the execution of that death sentence will be to plead his case before the state governor or, if it is a federal death sentence, before the United States President. The truly "legal" challenges to a death sentence occur only in the courts, both trial and appellate, and the clemency petition to the governor is essentially a plea for mercy despite having had all of the purely legal rulings go the other way.

The typical clemency process requires that the death row inmate's lawyers file the clemency petition with a state board (appointed by the governor), often the same board that handles parole petitions from prisoners serving life sentences. This board reviews the written petition and also may hear oral testimony from the attorneys on both sides, from members of the victim's family, and from members of the offender's family. The board's final action is to send a recommendation to the governor which usually is advisory but which, in states such as Texas, may bind the governor's hands in considering a grant of clemency.

State governors traditionally wait until almost the last day in deciding whether to grant clemency to a death row inmate scheduled for execution. Clemency decisions are intensely political decisions, being made by political leaders beholden to the voting public for their present jobs and often hoping to return to that voting public either for reelection to that same office or for election to a new office.

Mercy and justice undoubtedly are part of their consideration, but they play a minor role in comparison to political considerations. If the governor grants clemency, typically the offender's death sentence is changed to life in prison without parole. If the governor does not grant clemency, then execution is imminent.

Execution follows only the governor's signing of a death warrant, essentially an executive order from the governor to the prison warden to execute prisoner John Doe on or before a certain date. Prison officials then put into motion a carefully planned and well-rehearsed process to carry out this order. Almost all jurisdictions today use lethal injection as the governmental means of terminating the prisoner's life, although the history of execution techniques down through the ages includes a wide array of bizarre and ghastly means of dispatching the condemned (see chapter 1).

While executions are no longer public, a few witnesses to the execution are selected from the victim's family, the offender's family, the press, and governmental officials. The execution takes place inside the maximum security prison, and the entire occasion is a solemn procedure. Often one sees animated demonstrations outside the prison by groups in favor of or opposed to the execution, but inside the prison all is quiet and decorous. The witnesses are permitted to see only the few minutes needed for the actual termination of life and not all of the days of elaborate preparations. Once the prisoner is dead, his or her remains are given to the family of the deceased or, if none are available, may be buried in a prison cemetery or a potter's field somewhere nearby.

In the current death penalty era (1973–present), only about 14% of all persons sentenced to death have actually been executed. Some of the others have "cheated the executioner" by dying of suicide, murder, or natural causes, but many have simply had their death sentences reversed and were relegated to prison sentences. However, almost half of all persons sentenced to death in the current era are still on death row, continuing to challenge their death sentence but realizing that some day their time may come as well.

CHAPTER 9

JURY SELECTION AND ROLE OF JURORS

Unlike almost all other criminal cases, death penalty cases require the trial jury to determine the life-or-death sentence. Following the guilty-or-not-guilty trial stage, the same jury sits through a second evidentiary hearing focused solely on whether the now-convicted offender should be sentenced to death or to life imprisonment. Knowing that this jury must be both neutral concerning whether the defendant was involved in the crime and also be able to choose either sentence alternative, jurors are selected prior to the guilt stage with an eye toward their ability ultimately to vote for the death sentence if need be. Death penalty cases tend to be long, emotional, and complicated criminal proceedings, replete with tense and difficult considerations, and death penalty juries are at the epicenter. What greater responsibility can a public citizen be asked to shoulder than whether a fellow human being is to be put to death by government authorities?

§ 9.1 History and Power of Death Penalty Juries

The central role played by trial juries in Anglo–American criminal law is centuries old and remains extremely strong. The 6th Amendment, made applicable to the states by the 14th Amendment, includes a list of rights of the accused in all criminal prosecutions, including "the right to a speedy and public trial, by an impartial jury of the State and district where the crime shall have been committed...." This fundamental constitutional right to trial by jury has been constricted somewhat in criminal prosecutions of less seriousness, but it has remained in full bloom for death penalty cases. In fact, the Supreme Court has held that the aggravating circumstances upon which a death sentence is based must be found by the jury and not just by the trial judge. *Ring v. Arizona*, 536 U.S. 584, 122 S.Ct. 2428, 153 L.Ed.2d 556 (2002).

This awesome, ultimate power over the very life of the defendant is given over to an ad hoc collection of local citizens with no training or experience in such matters. Selection of this jury begins first with putting together a list of potential jurors using voter registration rolls, telephone directories, and/or other sources. The operating assumption is that this jury list is broadly representative of the community in which the crime was committed. From the jury list, a venire or panel is selected (typically at random) to be summoned and appear for jury duty. The venire will not perfectly reflect the community, as people are weeded out due to a variety of valid excuses for being unavailable to serve on this jury.

The trial judge and the lawyers on either side then select the trial jury from the venire. Through a process called *voir dire*, the prospective jurors are questioned and may be challenged or accepted, all in an effort to get down to a final 12–member jury and a few alternates. The prosecution and defense attorneys each can eliminate potential jurors through peremptory challenges without giving any reasons, but the number of peremptory challenges available to each side is limited. The attorneys also have unlimited numbers of challenges "for cause," but they must be able to convince the trial judge that the prospective juror is either legally disqualified or would be unable to decide the case in an unbiased and impartial manner. The special concerns in selecting death penalty juries are described in §§ 9.2, 9.3, and 9.4.

Once the trial jury is selected, the trial judge gives them some opening words of welcome and guidance, the lawyers make their opening statements, and the death penalty trial is off and running. As the Supreme Court made clear in *Ring*, the jury is the all-important player in death penalty cases. The other actors are fully aware of the centrality of the jury, and they orient all critical aspects of the case toward those 12 jurors.

§ 9.2 Death–Qualifying Juries

Selecting 12 actual jurors from the list of perhaps hundreds of names on a venire is a daunting task, sometimes consuming days or weeks of court time. Death penalty juries, as with any criminal trial jury, must be composed of jurors who are not friends or family members of the defendant, victim, judge, or lawyers, are not already biased in favor of one side or the other, are able to sit through a probably long and tedious trial and sentencing hearing, and are generally able to pass muster in numerous other ways. A criminal trial jury is thought of as the "conscience of the community" and should reflect that community broadly and accurately. This is particularly critical in death penalty law, given its foundation upon the "evolving standards of decency that mark the progress of a maturing society." *Trop v. Dulles*, 356 U.S. 86, 78 S.Ct. 590, 2 L.Ed.2d 630 (1958).

However, selecting death penalty juries has additional, very serious challenges. The members of this jury will first sit through the guilt stage of the proceedings, sifting through evidence and arguments to determine whether they can conclude, beyond a reasonable doubt, that a particular crime was committed and that this specific defendant committed that particular crime. This effort requires a careful ability to comprehend and weigh facts, to know which witnesses are telling the truth and which ones probably are not, and to put all of those findings into a final conclusion as to guilt.

All of this is the same as for any criminal trial jury, but if the defendant is convicted of a capital offense, then the death penalty jury must move onto a second, quite different stage, unlike that faced by other criminal trial juries. At the sentencing stage, the jury once again sifts through evidence and arguments and weighs the credibility of witnesses but toward a quite different end. After sitting through this sentencing stage and concluding which if any aggravating and mitigating circumstances have been proven, the death penalty jury must decide literally whether this defendant should live or die. It is up to the jury whether the defendant is sentenced to death or to the only other alternative, life in prison. This sentencing decision goes beyond finding facts and coming to conclusions from those facts. Death sentencing asks juries to play God.

It is different focuses of these two, quite different roles we ask death penalty juries to perform that generate so much difficulty and concern in selecting individual jurors to make up those juries. Even before they have heard any evidence in the case, and certainly before they have decided that the defendant committed the crime, prospective jurors are grilled on whether or not they would be willing to sentence the defendant to death. Determining this willingness to impose a death sentence has been given the macabre label of "death qualifying" the jury, essentially selecting a jury which would be able to return a death verdict if and when appropriate.

After a quarter century of establishing the boundaries of the selection process for capital juries, a line of United States Supreme Court cases has outlined what we need to know about prospective jurors' views on the death penalty. The line starts in 1968 with *Witherspoon v. Illinois*, 391 U.S. 510, 88 S.Ct. 1770, 20 L.Ed.2d 776 (1968). This remains a major case today even though it preceded by several years the complete revamping of the death penalty system by *Furman v. Georgia*, 408 U.S. 238, 92 S.Ct. 2726, 33 L.Ed.2d 346 (1972) and *Gregg v. Georgia*, 428 U.S. 153, 96 S.Ct. 2909, 49 L.Ed.2d 859 (1976) the prosecutor had been able to use unlimited challenges to exclude any and all prospective jurors who "might hesitate" to sentence a defendant to death. Those who made the cut were those with no "qualms about capital punishment." The Supreme Court in *Witherspoon* dubbed this "a hanging jury" and "a jury uncommonly willing to condemn a man to die." Perhaps not surprisingly, this trial jury had convicted the defendant of murder and had readily sentenced him to death.

Witherspoon found that the 6th Amendment right to an impartial jury, imposed upon the states through the 14th Amendment's due process requirement, does not permit the execution of a person pursuant to the verdict of a jury composed of jurors selected in such a slanted manner. Prospective jurors cannot be excluded "simply because they voiced general objections to the death penalty or expressed conscientious or religious scruples against its infliction." And, according to *Witherspoon*, prospective jurors cannot be expected to predict in advance whether they would impose the death penalty in the case about to be tried. Coming at this from the other end of the spectrum, *Witherspoon* noted that prospective jurors could be excluded if (1) they would automatically vote against a death sentence regardless of the evidence in the case or (2) they could not make an impartial decision as to guilt because of their attitudes toward the death penalty. Prospective jurors still eligible to serve on a death penalty jury after *Witherspoon* would be those in between these two extreme ends of the spectrum. This principle was reaffirmed in Uttecht v. Brown, ___ U.S. ___, 127 S.Ct. 2218, 167 L.Ed.2d 1014 (2007). These exclusions of prospective jurors considered under *Witherspoon* result from challenges for cause. Under the much more vague and obscure peremptory challenges, the challenging attorney need not give a reason. One suspects that some prospective jurors who were not quite excludable under *Witherspoon*'s constitutional challenges for cause might be sent on their way as a result of a nonspecific peremptory challenge.

In the decade following *Witherspoon* in 1968, death penalty law survived earthshaking challenges and changes. Essentially the only significant death penalty case that emerged largely intact after the 1970's was *Witherspoon*, still good law into the twenty-first century. Of course, the principles of *Witherspoon* still were challenged by both sides and continued to be shaped by the Supreme Court. *Adams v. Texas*, 448 U.S. 38, 100 S.Ct. 2521, 65 L.Ed.2d 581 (1980), held that prospective jurors could not be excluded under *Witherspoon* simply because they admitted they would be "affected by" the possibility of a death sentence. The Supreme Court in *Adams* held that an excludable juror must hold views that "would prevent or substantially impair the performance of his duties as a juror in accordance with the instructions and his oath." These duties include choosing carefully between either the death sentence or life imprisonment, so a juror must be able to make that choice without "substantial impairment."

A few years later, the Supreme Court upheld *Adams* and clarified *Witherspoon* with its decision in *Witherspoon*. Chief Justice Rehnquist's majority opinion in *Witt* limited somewhat the more expansive language in *Witherspoon* and strongly endorsed the holding in *Adams*. A prospective juror does not have to be automatically opposed to the death penalty to be challenged for cause, but the *Adams* test remains whether the prospective juror's views would "prevent or substantially impair the performance of his [or her] duties." The Supreme Court, again per Chief Justice Rehnquist, put the final touches on this issue in *Lockhart v. McCree*, 476 U.S. 162, 106 S.Ct. 1758, 90 L.Ed.2d 137 (1986). Death penalty trial courts can continue to death-qualify juries, and the results will satisfy the need for a fair cross-section of the community. However, a death sentence can be nullified if even a single prospective member of the death penalty jury was excluded improperly by the prosecution. *Gray v. Mississippi*, 481 U.S. 648, 107 S.Ct. 2045, 95 L.Ed.2d 622 (1987); *Uttecht v. Brown*, ___ U.S. ___, 127 S.Ct. 2218, 167 L.Ed.2d 1014 (2007).

§ 9.3 Life–Qualifying Juries and Other Concerns

The overriding concern in the death-qualification of juries is to select a jury that can and will give serious consideration to both sentence alternatives, life and death, and then choose the sentence that is best for the case at hand. The *Adams* test allows us to exclude those whose views would "prevent or substantially impair" their ability to do this, driven by a state concern that some jurors might not be able to impose a death sentence. The defendant typically has the opposite concern, that some prospective jurors might always impose a death sentence and never impose life imprisonment. This might be dubbed a "life qualifying" or "reverse-*Witherspoon*" issue.

The right for a capital defendant to life-qualify prospective jurors was granted in *Morgan v. Illinois*, 504 U.S. 719, 112 S.Ct. 2222, 119 L.Ed.2d 492 (1992). In *Morgan*, the trial judge had questioned prospective jurors as to any "substantial doubts" about their ability to impose the death sentence, striking several because of such doubts. However, the trial judge refused to ask the prospective jurors whether they would "automatically vote to impose the death penalty no matter what the facts are." The Supreme Court in *Morgan* provided a mirror image to *Witherspoon* in holding that a juror who would always vote for the death penalty would be failing to follow the instructions and oath of death penalty jurors to carefully weigh the aggravating and mitigating circumstances and only then to decide between life and death for the convicted murderer. The defendant has a 6th Amendment right to an impartial jury, and jurors are not impartial if they would automatically vote either for death or for life without considering the evidence presented in the sentencing hearing.

The end result of the death qualifying cases and the life qualifying cases is that both ends of the spectrum are truncated. The remaining prospective jurors still qualified for final selection to the death penalty jury are those views about the death penalty would neither automatically cause them to choose death, regardless of the facts of the case, nor substantially impair them from choosing death, should the facts of the case warrant it. True to a fundamental premise of the modern death penalty system, the members of a death penalty jury must not have made their minds up, one way or the other, before the case even begins.

A particularly troublesome issue that kept arising in the death-qualification cases was the specter of "conviction-prone" juries. Considerable empirical research indicates that juries selected so that they can impose a death penalty if needed may also be inherently more likely to convict the defendant originally at the guilt stage. That is, that part of society that favors the death penalty tends also to include an inordinate percentage of persons who are more likely than the average person to believe the police and prosecutor side of the case, to discount the defense side, and to convict defendants at trial. If this research is correct, such "conviction-prone" juries would violate the defendant's right to an impartial jury representative of a cross-section of the community. However, the Supreme Court in several of these cases, most particularly in *McCree*, did not find this research sufficiently convincing in these cases to alter their holdings.

This research continues to be conducted and is fairly convincing. However, the cure for this problem may be seen as worse than the disease. If death qualified juries are in fact conviction-prone (and perhaps even if life qualified juries might be acquittal-prone), then the obvious solution is to limit such juries solely to the sentencing stage of the trial-level process. Select another jury to hear and decide the guilt stage, one for which the issues of death penalty viewpoint would be less central to the assigned task. The costs of such a solution are to go through the jury selection process twice, slogging down long *venire* lists to get to the final composite of 12 plus alternates. In addition to doubling the selection process, this alternative would also require nearly doubling the information and education process for the sentencing stage jury. In the current system, with one trial jury sitting for the entire case, this jury begins the sentencing stage with detailed information about the crime the defendant has committed. This crime information is a critical part of the sentencing decision. If a new jury is chosen for the sentencing stage following conviction, then the first part of the sentencing hearing would have to be devoted to going over information about the crime from the guilt stage. Not surprisingly, no death penalty jurisdiction has chosen this two-jury alternative.

Another solution to the conviction prone jury problem implemented by a handful of death penalty states was to put the entire sentencing process and decision before the trial judge. Following conviction, the trial jury was dismissed and sent home, with the subsequent sentencing being handled solely by the judge. In addition to greatly simplifying the jury selection process, this model allowed the sentencing hearing to be conducted some time after the guilt stage had been completed and even in a series of installments as witnesses and evidence became available. The essentially conclusive presumption is that the trial judge can and will make a reasoned choice between life or death. However, the Supreme Court put an end to this option with its decision in *Ring v. Arizona*, 536 U.S. 584, 122 S.Ct. 2428, 153 L.Ed.2d 556 (2002). The critical findings and the death sentence itself must be the work of the jury, not the judge, so we are back to the original problem apparently without viable alternatives.

§ 9.4 Other Jury Concerns

A very common problem in selecting a jury for a death penalty case is that the crimes which lead to such prosecutions tend to receive considerable newspaper and television coverage from the moment they are discovered. Particularly given the media's insatiable appetite for stories about violent crime, sensational murders are nearly guaranteed to be headline news for long periods of time. Prospective jurors will come from that same community, so finding people who are totally unaware of this adverse media coverage would be nearly impossible.

Consider the impact of the fairly uniform bias of our judges and juries in favor of the death penalty. Almost all American judges are elected, with the few others being appointed by political office holders who themselves are elected. Being perceived as tough on crime is considered necessary for political success, so essentially every death penalty judge has achieved office in part because of a stated willingness, even eagerness, to severely punish criminal offenders. Juries, likewise, are selected from a general population that is strongly in favor of the death penalty. While those with extreme views on either end of the spectrum are eliminated, the jury's views generally represent those of the community, and that includes a widespread pro-death penalty view. Attempts have been made to neutralize this bias but with limited success.

The Supreme Court's discussion of death-qualifying a capital jury, along with the broad issue of selecting a fair and impartial jury in criminal cases, provides a context for exploring other inherent biases held by prospective jurors in death penalty cases. As a beginning, the Supreme Court has established that capital defendants accused of interracial crimes are entitled to have prospective jurors questioned on the issue of race bias. *Turner v. Murray*, 476 U.S. 28, 106 S.Ct. 1683, 90 L.Ed.2d 27 (1986). The Supreme Court in *Turner* noted the particularly wide ranging power and discretion of trial juries in death penalty cases, providing a unique opportunity for racial prejudice to operate but remain undetected.

Racial bias in jury selection was also the issue in Snyder v. Louisiana, ___ U.S. ___, 128 S.Ct. 1203, 170 L.Ed.2d 175 (2008). There the prosecutor had used peremptory strikes in order to get an all-white jury for the black defendant. The Snyder court reversed the conviction due to this racial bias in rejecting potential jurors.

Turner involved a black robber who shot and killed a white storekeeper in Virginia, and the Supreme Court understood the fertile ground race bias might find in such a case. Similar issues might be raised as to gender bias, particularly in cases involving male offenders and/or female victims. Religious bias is another obvious concern, such as when the religion of the accused is unrepresented in the community and perhaps carries with it the baggage of association with terrorists or other targeted groups. A final example might be sexual orientation in a case of a gay defendant being tried in a very conservative Midwestern community.

Questions could be drafted to explore prospective jurors' views on many of these potential issues of bias, perhaps tailored to fit the facts of the particular case the jury would be deciding. The trial judge's final charge to the jury before they retire to deliberate upon life versus death might be influential in bringing such possible biases to the surface and causing the jury to deal with them directly. For example, the federal death penalty statute has put at least some of these potential biases on the table in requiring the trial judge to instruct the jury concerning them:

[T]he court ... shall instruct the jury that, in considering whether a sentence of death is justified, it shall not consider the race, color, religious beliefs, national origin, or sex of the defendant or of any victim ... 18 U.S.C. 3593(f)

When the jury in a federal capital case returns its sentencing recommendation in a capital case, each juror must sign a certificate verifying that these factors were not considered. This final requirement could be made clear even as prospective jurors are being questioned, so that these issues are on their minds from the very beginning of the case. Might not such federal requirements be worthwhile additions to proceedings in state death penalty cases?

CHAPTER 10

GUILT STAGE OF TRIAL PROCESS

Assume now that the defendant has been arrested for a capital crime, the prosecutor has levied death penalty charges, and the case is ready to go to trial. Chapter 9 described the complex procedure of selecting a jury to sit for this trial, but now we should be ready to proceed. Before going through the several trial issues in death penalty cases, this chapter will set the stage, particularly as to the key players at this trial. Then we move to the two major stages or functions of the guilt stage: the evidence presented by the state and the evidence presented by the defense. The final scene is that portrayed in countless books and films. The jury returns to the courtroom and announces its verdict: guilty or not guilty.

§ 10.1 Defendants, Defense Attorneys, Prosecutors, and Judges

On the opening day of trial, the jury, the spectators, and the representatives of the press will focus first on the defendant, on trial for his life. Almost always male, typically under age 25, and more likely than not to be a person of color, the capital defendant at trial may not look much like the fleeting photographs taken when he was arrested or his mug shot taken during booking. The trial will commence about a year or so after those earlier events, but it is not just the passage of time that changes the defendant and his appearance.

Since the day of his arrest, the capital defendant will have been incarcerated in the local jail, awaiting trial. His chances of having been released on bail pending trial are essentially zero. As the defendant and his defense team prepare legal strategies and tactics for the two-stage trial, the defendant also is molded and shaped in preparation for this signal public performance. To the degree to which the defendant will permit it, the defense team works to modify the defendant's appearance and demeanor to make a more favorable impression upon the jury and, to some degree, upon the judge.

Capital defendants almost never actually testify at the guilt stage of the trial process, but "all eyes will be on him" as the case progresses. Jurors will read hostility, remorse, defiance, mental incompetence, and/or other abilities and attitudes into the defendant's gestures, eye contact, manner of dress, hairstyle, and general facial expressions. As we are only at the very beginning of the guilt stage, the unspoken issue floating throughout the courtroom is whether the defendant is to live or to die. As the jury tries to decide if the defendant has even committed any crimes which would put his life in jeopardy, they are trying to "take the measure of the man" at the defense table. This truism is the motivation for the defense team to have altered the defendant's appearance to conform to community norms and to have coached the defendant as to the most beneficial demeanor and behavior in which to engage in the presence of the jury.

Sitting next to the defendant at the defense table is the defense attorney, along with perhaps co-counsel and/or a defense investigator. The entire defense team may be just one overwhelmed criminal lawyer or, in some jurisdictions, the defense team may include two criminal lawyers, a defense investigator, and a mitigation specialist. However, the member of this defense team who plays a prominent role in the guilt stage is the defense attorney. If two attorneys are assigned to the case, typically one will be lead counsel for the guilt stage and the other will be lead counsel for the sentencing stage. In any event, the jury, judge, and other observers will see and hear from a single defense attorney.

Since very few capital defendants have sufficient funds to hire a private attorney to represent them, the vast majority of defense lawyers in death penalty cases are local public defenders. Death cases are the most important and the most complex, so typically they are assigned to the most experienced trial litigators in the public defender's office. If no public defender office exists, or if the public defender is precluded from taking the case due to conflicts with other public defender clients, it is common for the trial judge to appoint a private criminal defense attorney to represent the capital defendant, paid a set fee by the court and not by the defendant. In any event, they almost always are lawyers in and of the local community, familiar in appearance and demeanor to the local jury members and the local judge. Because the jury will almost never hear from the defendant himself, it is the appearance, voice, and general presence of the defense attorney that will characterize "the defense" in the minds of the jurors, the judge, the spectators, and the press.

Sitting at the other table in front of the judge's bench will be the prosecuting attorney, labeled in some jurisdictions the district attorney, the parish attorney, or the people's attorney. The lead counsel from the prosecutor's office may be accompanied by the chief (elected) prosecutor, by an investigator intimately familiar with the facts of the crime investigation, and perhaps, even by a member of the victim's family. Remember that a death penalty trial is a major event within that local criminal justice system, and the chief prosecutor is an elected political official who is a major player within the local criminal justice system. Therefore, while the chief prosecutor will want the office's most accomplished criminal trial lawyer to actually try the case, this elected political official would rarely pass up the opportunity to make a public appearance at such an event. However, the "voice" of the government in this death penalty trial will be the lead counsel from the prosecutor's office (prosecuting attorney).

Last but certainly not least, the trial judge sits up higher than all of the others, behind a comparatively large bench or dais, clearly somewhat removed from the fray. However, it is the trial judge who serves both as the traffic cop when the evidence is being presented and as the source of law (and wisdom?) for the jury. The jury will hear fairly lengthy statements from the judge at the beginning and end of the guilt stage, as well as briefer words of guidance during the proceedings. The trial judge is acutely aware that even the slightest missteps (or the appearance of missteps) during these proceedings will be chronicled in the appellate proceedings, so death penalty trial judges may be even more careful about dotting every "i" and crossing every "t" as they move through the trial process.

Trial judges in death penalty cases are also political officials, usually elected locally or sometimes appointed by other officials who are elected. Candidates for election, reelection, or appointment to a trial court judgeship in death penalty states are anxious to be seen as major players in death penalty cases. Whether or not the trial court allows cameras in the courtroom, the trial court judge is well aware of the intense media interest in death penalty trials and that the judge's name and courtroom will figure prominently in these high-profile media reports in the local community. A stern, dignified, "tough-on-crime" image of the judge projected at a death penalty trial will be very helpful during the next election, and any hint of an anti-death penalty leaning will provide fertile opportunities for opponents to exploit. Public officials are sensitive to their public images at public events, and the zenith of this principle for local trial court judges are death penalty trials in their courtrooms.

The other people who have filled the courtroom for a death penalty trial include a variety of uniformed bailiffs and police officers there to insure order and security. Friends and family of the victim can be expected to fill several seats, often with the widow dressed in black sitting prominently in the front row. If the victim was a police officer, the spectator seats often are filled with police officers in full dress uniform. The defendant's family typically is also represented, perhaps only by his mother or minister. The other seats are filled by representatives of the press and by other interested members of the community. None of this is lost on the jurors, as they scan the courtroom trying to figure out who this person or that person might be. Members of local political action groups are well aware of the quiet power of their presence in the courtroom, and one tends to see them out in force at death penalty trials.

§ 10.2   State's Evidence

After the case has been announced and the judge has welcomed the jury and explained some basic ground rules, the prosecuting attorney begins to make the state's case. The legal posture at the outset of the guilt stage of a death penalty trial is that the defendant is "innocent until proven guilty," so the prosecuting attorney has the affirmative responsibility to prove that the alleged crime (and all of its elements) actually occurred and that this particular defendant committed that specific crime. Even more demanding, the Supreme Court has interpreted 14th Amendment due process to require that all of this must be proven beyond a reasonable doubt before the defendant can be convicted. *In re Winship*, 397 U.S. 358, 90 S.Ct. 1068, 25 L.Ed.2d 368 (1970).

As mentioned in § 8.2, nearly a year of pretrial skirmishes will have preceded this opening moment of the guilt stage of a death penalty trial. A key result of these skirmishes is that the prosecuting attorney now knows what items of the state's evidence will be admissible at trial for the jury to take into consideration. Any items of evidence (extracted confessions, seized weapons, etc.) that are inadmissable have already been excluded by the trial judge as a result of an earlier evidence suppression hearing, and the prosecuting attorney then builds the state's case around the remaining evidence that can be presented at trial. Another probable result of the pretrial activities is that the prosecuting attorney knows the primary defenses the defendant plans to use, so the state's case can be molded to address those anticipated defenses. Finally, the prosecuting attorney knows that the defendant is not willing (at least so far) to enter a plea bargain and to plead guilty to this crime or to another crime offered by the state, so now the state must take the case to court.

Another key issue that grows from the state's pretrial gathering of evidence can be a reluctant concession for the state and/or a boon for the defense. If the prosecutor learns of evidence favorable to the defense, that evidence must be turned over to the defense as soon as possible. *Brady v. Maryland*, 373 U.S. 83, 83 S.Ct. 1194, 10 L.Ed.2d 215 (1963). *Brady* required that such pro-defense evidence be relevant and material either to guilt or to punishment, and subsequent cases have required that such *Brady* evidence constitute a reasonable probability that, if disclosed to the defense, a different result would have occurred. *United States v. Bagley*, 473 U.S. 667, 105 S.Ct. 3375, 87 L.Ed.2d 481 (1985). Therefore, a part of the prosecuting attorney's responsibility is to reveal evidence to the defense.

The state begins its case with an opening statement to the jury. The prosecuting attorney uses this opening statement both as a preview of coming attractions and as a means of providing the jury an overview of the state's theory of the case. In many cases, the prosecuting attorney's opening statement to the jury is followed immediately by a similar opening statement by the defense attorney. In other cases, the defense attorney's opening statement may be delayed until all of the state's evidence has been presented.

Following the opening statement(s), the prosecuting attorney presents the state's evidence-in-chief. The state's evidence almost always includes the sworn testimony of witnesses, including private citizens who may have seen some of the events in question, police officers who investigated the crime, medical professionals who examined the deceased victim, and other experts who have special knowledge. In addition to the testimony of witnesses, the state will introduce and rely upon physical evidence, such as weapons, clothing, documents, photographs, etc. Almost always, this physical evidence will be introduced during the testimony of the witnesses who verify the identity and relevance of these tangible items.

Typically the state's major thrust is to prove that the crime actually occurred. In death penalty cases, the crime(s) tend to be particularly horrible and sensational. The jury will hear about the gruesome crime scene, learn the medical details of how the victim(s) died, and, most significantly, see several detailed photographs of the crime scene, the victim(s), and the general mayhem resulting from this crime. Even putting aside any evidence connecting this particular defendant to the crime, the jury will be shocked and angered by the facts of the crime and will want retribution against those responsible. The defendant's mere presence in the courtroom gives the jury a personal focus for its anger, and the "innocent until proven guilty" premise begins to crumble.

To be sure, the state's evidence will also make every effort to connect this defendant to this crime. In some cases, this is not too difficult, with videotape of the crime, eyewitnesses' identifications, DNA evidence, and the defendant's confession. In other cases, very little evidence is introduced to prove that this defendant committed this crime, with heavy reliance upon the questionable evidence of eyewitness identification and the defendant's confession. In these latter cases, the jury runs the risk of combining its outrage over the horrible crime with its desire to punish the perpetrator of this horrible crime. This combination can be deadly for a defendant who is not strongly connected by the evidence to the crime but is the "apparent" or "most likely" perpetrator. If the jury sees its choice as convicting either this defendant or convicting no one for this terrible crime, the jury may be tempted to rely too heavily on thin evidence and convict the defendant.

In a death penalty case, the guilt stage typically requires only the evidence needed to convict the defendant of the crime. The assumption is that evidence as to the appropriate sentence would become relevant only if and when the defendant is convicted of the crime at the guilt stage of the trial process and then enters the sentencing stage. However, the state's goal is to provide evidence to the jury that the defendant is death-eligible. This is accomplished in some jurisdictions by proving the defendant guilty of a capital crime at the guilt stage, including proof of the elements of the crime that make it a capital crime and therefore make the defendant death-eligible. Other jurisdictions save all or most of this aspect of the state's case until the sentencing hearing.

Whether or not the prosecuting attorney is required to present evidence during the guilt stage to make the defendant death-eligible, this end goal is nonetheless a continuing theme. For example, the prosecuting attorney will not just try to convince the jury that the defendant committed a murder, but additional evidence will be presented to demonstrate how shocking and outrageous this particular murder actually was. Such additional evidence seldom has any functional use in getting the actual conviction at hand, but it may provide a significance boost to the state in getting a death penalty verdict later on in the trial process (see chapter 11). Remember that this is the same jury that will be considering a sentence of life or death immediately following a conviction, so the prosecuting attorney begins working on them to this end even at the earliest stages of the guilt stage of the trial process.

At the close of the state's evidence, the prosecuting attorney may have the option of making a closing statement, summarizing the case against the defendant. However, this final closing argument usually is reserved until the very end of all evidence, both for the state and for the defense. Whenever it is made, the prosecutor's closing argument is a critical part of the state's case. It is the last word the jury will hear from the state before retiring to decide the defendant's guilt, so the prosecutor makes it memorable and emotional, sometimes a little too emotional.

One of the most infamous cases of a prosecutor's overzealousness in closing argument is *Darden v. Wainwright*, 477 U.S. 168, 106 S.Ct. 2464, 91 L.Ed.2d 144 (1986). There the prosecutor was somewhat tempted into rhetorical excess by the defense, but in any event the prosecuting attorney referred to the defendant as "this animal," said he "shouldn't be out of his cell unless he has a leash on him," and said he wished someone had blown the defendant's face and head off with a shotgun. Although every court that reviewed the *Darden* prosecutor's closing argument readily characterized it as improper, undesirable, and "universally condemned," no court (including the Supreme Court) found that such a closing argument deprived the defendant of a fair trial under 14th Amendment due process. If even a "universally condemned" closing argument results in only a tongue lashing such as this, one wonders what restraint, other than professional ethics, might cause a prosecuting attorney to tone down the closing argument. In *Darden*, the prosecutor's closing argument, in combination with the state's other evidence, was successful in getting the defendant convicted, sentenced to death, and executed.

§ 10.3 Defense Evidence

At the guilt stage of the trial process, the range of possible approaches for the defense is quite broad. At the risk of oversimplification, consider three categories of defense approaches. First, in some cases the defense has substantial evidence to challenge the state's assertion that the defendant actually committed the crime, trying to raise at least a "reasonable doubt" in the mind of the jury and thereby hope to gain an acquittal. In a second, more common category, the defense does not seriously challenge the state's evidence that the defendant committed the acts which constitute the crime. Instead, the defense effort is focused on a special issue such as the defendant's legal sanity. In a third category of defense approaches, neither of the key factors in the first two options is available. Here, the strategy is twofold: (1) hope for an error or omission by the state, and (2) prepare the jury for a more receptive sentencing hearing.

The first option is not unlike swinging from your heels for a home run, knowing that the alternative possibility is striking out and falling on your face. Here, the defense is asking the jury to accept their argument that the defendant didn't do it, that it is all a case of mistaken identity. If successful, the defendant is acquitted and walks away a free man. However, if the jury rejects this view of the events, they both convict the defendant and characterize his guilt-stage arguments as lies and fabrications. When the same defendant comes before them the next day as the sentencing hearing begins, the jury is predisposed to see the defendant (and the defense attorney) as less than candid and honest. This places a serious taint on the defense as it presents evidence and makes arguments at the sentencing hearing. Nonetheless, the Supreme Court's unanimous decision in *Holmes v. South Carolina*, 547 U.S. 319, 126 S.Ct. 1727, 164 L.Ed.2d 503 (2006) makes it clear that the defendant has every right to raise an argument of another party's guilt. Being able to compare the evidence of the defendant's guilt against the evidence of another party's guilt would seem to be basic requirement of proof beyond a reasonable doubt. *In re Winship*, 397 U.S. 358, 90 S.Ct. 1068, 25 L.Ed.2d 368 (1970).

The second option of not challenging the acts of the crime but claiming a special defense such as legal insanity is often the better choice for a capital defendant. If the state stumbles in proving the elements of the crime and the defendant's central involvement in that crime, the defense can simply draw that omission to the trial judge's attention and ask for a directed verdict of acquittal. If the state successfully proves its case, at least the defendant is not accused of lies and fabrications in denying the allegations. The primary effort of the defense attorney is to prove a defense such as legal insanity, and either outcome here has its positive dimensions. If the defendant is found not guilty by reason of insanity, he or she is committed to a mental hospital for the criminally insane but is not given a death sentence. Even if the jury does not agree with the insanity defense, at least the defense has gotten ample evidence of the defendant's mental problems before the jury. This same issue can be revisited at the sentencing hearing under a variety of mitigating circumstances dealing with a convicted murderer's mental problems, working toward avoiding a death sentence even if convicted.

The third option is in essence to stand on a defendant's right to have the case proven by the state beyond a reasonable doubt. No major obstacles are thrown in the path of the prosecuting attorney, but the defense attorney simply watches like a hawk, ready to swoop down and scream about any error or omission. The state's evidence is tested at every opportunity, hoping to find a weakness or a flaw.

By neither denying the charges nor pushing for some "clever excuse" defense such as legal insanity, the defendant minimizes the risk of alienating the jury (beyond the alienation that comes from having committed murder!). Another, perhaps more important benefit can be a defendant's methodical and consistent effort to lay the groundwork for a favorable sentencing hearing. The defense essentially concedes conviction of a capital crime and focuses almost entirely upon avoiding a death sentence. This approach involves not only the avoidance of annoying the jury with misleading claims but also the insertion of themes and evidence throughout the guilt stage to which the defense will return during the sentencing stage. Typical examples might be the defendant's peripheral involvement in the crime or the victim's precipitation of his own death.

According to the approach chosen by the defense attorney, more or less emphasis will be placed upon the defendant's case-in-chief presented after the state's evidence is completed. If the defense is either that the defendant was in Albuquerque at the time the crime was committed in Albany, or that the defendant's mental problems add up to legal insanity, then a substantial amount of physical and testimonial evidence may be necessary. However, if no such affirmative defense is chosen, the defense attorney may have little if any direct evidence to present. In all of these circumstances, the defense attorney can be expected to cross-examine the state's witnesses where helpful to the defense. Sometimes this is done simply to test the validity and assuredness of this testimony, and sometimes the goal is to lay the groundwork for a guilt stage defense to be made or a sentencing stage argument to be pursued if the defendant is convicted.

Once the defendant's direct evidence is completed, then the prosecution has a right to respond to the defense evidence with rebuttal evidence. The goal here usually is to challenge some special point the defense has made, such as a legal insanity defense. If the prosecution's rebuttal evidence raise new issues, then the defense will have a similar right to present evidence to rebut the rebuttal evidence.

Both sides then move to their closing arguments. As discussed in § 10.2 for the prosecuting attorney, this is the last opportunity for the two lawyers to make their cases to the jury. The defense attorney's closing argument both points out the weak points of the state's case and summarizes any special defenses made. The defendant has almost never actually testified at the guilt stage, so the defense attorney may personify the defense sometimes even more than the defendant himself. The defense attorney's goal, therefore, is both to outline the path to end results favorable to the defendant and to impress the jury as an honest and reliable person.

§ 10.4 Jury Verdict

Following this presentation of evidence and argument to the jury, they are instructed by the trial judge as to the law to be applied in the case. While the two attorneys may have referred to the requirements of the law in their arguments to the jury, it is the trial judge who is the sole official source of the law for the jury. They "receive" this law via formal jury instructions, read to the jury by the judge after all evidence has been presented. These jury instructions often are not easily understood by lay persons in large part because they have been drafted by lawyers.

The jury then retires to the jury room to decide, beyond a reasonable doubt, whether the defendant is guilty of the crime(s) as charged. Juries typically work from a suggested schedule, including picking a jury foreman, discussing the evidence, taking straw polls as to possible verdicts, and finally reaching a final verdict upon which all 12 jurors can agree. These jury deliberations can consume from a few hours to many days, as the defendant waits in a holding cell and the lawyers stay close to a telephone or intercom.

It is not uncommon for a jury to be unable to reach unanimous agreement on a verdict, and they report this to the trial judge. The judge need not dismiss the jury at the first sign of deadlock, and a variety of efforts might be made to help them see their way to agreement. Particularly given the enormous time, effort, and expense of death penalty trials, judges are very reluctant to find a jury deadlocked, to dismiss that jury, and to force the state to start all over again.

Assuming that the jury can and does reach a unanimous conclusion, the 12 jurors return to the trial courtroom where all of the other key players (defendant, defense attorney, prosecuting attorney, and judge, as well as interested spectators and the press) are reassembled. If the jury finds the defendant not guilty of any and all crimes, the case is dismissed and the defendant walks free. If the jury finds the defendant guilty of some lesser included crime(s) but not any of the capital crimes that were charged, the judge will enter the conviction(s), dismiss the jury, and order a noncapital sentencing hearing to be held solely in front of that judge at some time in the future. Either of these two scenarios terminates the death penalty dimension of the case, because no death penalty may now be imposed.

If the jury finds the defendant guilty of one or more capital crimes, then their work has not ended. Instead of being sent back to their families, their friends, their homes, and their jobs, these same 12 jurors must remain for the most challenging part of any death penalty case—the sentencing stage of the trial process.

CHAPTER 11

SENTENCING STAGE OF TRIAL PROCESS

The only unique parts of the death penalty system are the sentencing stage of the trial process and the actual execution of the condemned prisoner. It is here that the primary focus of the death penalty system comes into stark relief. This life-or-death sentencing decision is left to the trial jury, the same jury that sat through the guilt stage of the trial process and convicted the defendant of a capital crime. The sentencing hearing typically begins either immediately after the guilty verdict is announced or the next morning at the latest. The same trial jurors take their same seats in the same jury box in the same courtroom, and the same trial judge explains to them the quite different focus of this second hearing before them. Only about 2% of all murderers are sentenced to death, and less than 1% are actually executed. The responsibility of the death penalty system at this point is to decide if indeed this convicted murderer is among the "worst of the worst" and should be sentenced to death for his or her crimes.

§ 11.1   State's Evidence

During the guilt stage of the trial process, the prosecuting attorney typically carries the primary responsibility for bringing the case to the jury through witness testimony and physical evidence. Moving now to the sentencing stage, the primary burden of going forward shifts to the defense attorney. The role of the prosecuting attorney is much more modest in the sentencing stage, in that much of the state's argument in sentencing carries over from their success in the guilt stage. Seasoned death penalty prosecutors and defense attorneys know that juries tend to be "leaning toward death" at the beginning of the sentencing stage, so the role of the prosecuting attorney often is simply to maintain that momentum.

The decision to sentence the defendant to death must be based upon an analysis and evaluation of both the nature and circumstances of the crime and the character and background of the offender. *Gregg v. Georgia*, 428 U.S. 153, 96 S.Ct. 2909, 49 L.Ed.2d 859 (1976). Essentially all of the state's evidence concerning the nature and circumstances of the crime was presented at the guilt stage. Given that the defendant was convicted of the worst form of crime, a capital crime, the trial jury has already staked out its position concerning this first issue. Perhaps even more important, the same jurors who just completed their analysis of the crime are now sitting as the sentencing jury, so the evidence about the crime couldn't be fresher in their minds.

The prosecuting attorney launches the state's evidence portion of the sentencing stage with an opening statement to the jury, both reminding them of the evidence about the crime that they have just reviewed and forecasting for them the additional evidence they are about to see. When the prosecutor moves onto presenting hard evidence of aggravating circumstances, some of it may simply be restating what the jury has already found beyond a reasonable doubt. For example, a common aggravating circumstance is that the crime involved more than one murder victim. If this is true in this case, then the jury's earlier guilty verdict will already have established this aggravating circumstance. Similarly, if the victim was a police officer or if the homicide occurred along with another serious felony, these elements will already have been established at the guilt stage. Indeed, most aggravating circumstances are simply characteristics of the capital crime and therefore will be proven at the guilt stage. See § 6.2 for a discussion of common aggravating circumstances in death penalty statutes.

The new evidence as to aggravating circumstances to be presented by the state tends to focus on the character and background of the offender. Most common will be the past criminal record, if any, of the defendant in this case. This record will be particularly important if it includes past murders or other violent crimes. Introduction of this evidence is simple in most jurisdictions, with the prosecuting attorney simply bringing in the offender's record as verified by the department of corrections in the state(s) in which the prior convictions occurred. Other negative character evidence might also be available, but typically it will be reserved for use by the state in rebuttal should the defendant put on evidence of good character as to the same topics.

The state's grand finale in sentencing hearings often is choreographed around emotional evidence from the victim's family, commonly labeled a "victim impact statement" (VIS). This VIS evidence generally goes to the personal characteristics of the victim and to the emotional impact of the defendant's crimes on the victim's family. Often extremely emotional testimony will be taken from the victim's close friends and family members about the best characteristics of the victim and about the many ways in which the shock waves of the victim's murder have devastated the lives of those who knew and loved the victim. Sometimes this VIS evidence is simply a statement prepared outside and then read verbatim by the judge or by a family member to the jury at the sentencing stage of the trial process. Everyone in the courtroom, certainly including the members of the jury, feels the enormous pain and suffering of these individuals. The defense has almost no effective means to counter this evidence, even when the victim's life may not have been so saintly. One does not "speak ill of the dead," certainly not at the sentencing hearing of the murderer who inflicted that death.

The constitutionality of such evidence has taken a tortured path. The Supreme Court first held that the 8th Amendment prohibited a capital sentencing jury from considering VIS evidence. *Booth v. Mary-*

land, 482 U.S. 496, 107 S.Ct. 2529, 96 L.Ed.2d 440 (1987). The state in *Booth* argued that the VIS evidence simply informed the jury of the nature and circumstances of the crime, specifically as to its impact upon members of the victim's family. The defense countered that this was both irrelevant and unduly inflammatory evidence for a sentencing jury to hear. The *Booth* court thought that such evidence too greatly enhanced the risk of arbitrary and capricious action by the sentencing jury and ruled that all such evidence was barred by the Constitution unless it "relate[d] directly to the circumstances of the crime."

Soon thereafter, the Supreme Court decided *South Carolina v. Gathers*, 490 U.S. 805, 109 S.Ct. 2207, 104 L.Ed.2d 876 (1989). Here, in his closing statement at the sentencing stage, the prosecutor read at length from a religious tract found on the victim's body and inferred favorable personal qualities from this short prayer and from a voter's registration card also found on the victim. The Supreme Court in *Gathers* relied directly on *Booth* to hold that such personal characterizations of the victim were also prohibited by the 8th Amendment.

Two years later, the Supreme Court abruptly changed course, expressly overruled *Booth* and *Gathers*, and held that VIS evidence does not violate the 8th Amendment. *Payne v. Tennessee*, 501 U.S. 808, 111 S.Ct. 2597, 115 L.Ed.2d 720 (1991). The facts of *Payne* had been particularly horrific, including the multiple stabbing deaths of an infant and his mother. The mother's three–year-old son, Nicholas, was also stabbed as he witnessed the other murders, but he miraculously survived. The sad plight of Nicholas was stressed by the testimony of his grandmother, followed by the prosecutor's plea to the jury to return a death verdict as "something you can do for Nicholas."

The Supreme Court in *Payne* characterized the earlier holdings in *Booth* and *Gathers* as having been decided by the narrowest of margins over spirited dissents and as being questioned subsequently by members of the Supreme Court as well as other courts. While these characterizations of *Booth* and *Gathers* were true, they also would be true for many other cases, particularly in death penalty jurisprudence. In any event, *Payne* held that VIS evidence does not violate the 8th Amendment and is admissible as to the specific harm that resulted from the defendant's crime.

Following *Payne* in 1991, many death penalty states have seen either legislative or state supreme court action that now provides a vehicle for bringing in VIS evidence. If available to the prosecuting attorney, this VIS evidence will likely be the last item of evidence offered by the state at the sentencing stage of the trial process. It almost undoubtedly will be the most emotional pro-death evidence the jury will hear, and the defense has almost no way to counter it. Many death penalty prosecutors see VIS evidence as the knockout punch they need to get the result they seek.

The state's evidence actually concludes with the prosecuting attorney's closing argument, coming only after the defense has presented its sentencing evidence. These are the last words the prosecutor will ever speak to this jury, after having worked with them on a daily basis for days or perhaps weeks during this lengthy trial process. This is the same prosecutor who has already won a major victory with this jury in convincing them beyond a reasonable doubt that the defendant was guilty of a capital crime. Now the prosecutor is asking this same jury to do what the state wants again, to return a sentence of death for the murderer they convicted earlier. The prosecutor's closing argument at the end of the guilt stage was more methodical and point-by-point, but the prosecutor's closing argument at the end of the sentencing stage is more angry and emotional. The prosecutor can be expected to weave together themes of retribution, incapacitation, and deterrence, along with impassioned pleas from religious principles, cultural norms, and political philosophies. Major parts of the prosecuting attorney's job is to present a logical, methodical, and coherent case from beginning to end, leaving no important stone unturned. In striking contrast, this last part, the closing argument at the death sentencing hearing, is histrionic theater. However, the Supreme Court has imposed very few restrictions on this closing argument. Roper v. Weaver, ___ U.S. ___, 127 S.Ct. 2022, 167 L.Ed.2d 966 (2007).

§ 11.2 Defense Evidence

At the close of the state's evidence, often punctuated by the VIS evidence, the defense begins to put on its case for allowing the defendant to spend the rest of his life in prison, a grim alternative to being executed. Defense attorneys tend to face several obstacles in this endeavor even before they begin. First, always a few capital defendants will have decided that they would rather die than spend the rest of their lives in prison. This is not an uncommon conclusion for death row prisoners facing yet more years of uncertain appeals, but it also occurs even before the sentencing hearing has begun. This dilemma is discussed more completely in chapter 14, but the issue may also be relevant at this early stage. In essence, the defense attorney must decide whether to challenge the client's sanity (and thus the capability to make such a decision) or to simply abide by the client's wishes. It is not uncommon, however, for the trial judge to strongly encourage the defense counsel in such cases to bring as much evidence of mitigating circumstances forward as possible, so that the jury can make a reasonably informed and balanced decision. The mere fact that a person "wants to die" is not a sufficient reason for government officials to kill him.

A related but lesser version of the same issue comes up when the defendant refuses to authorize the defense attorney to put on certain kinds of evidence, despite the fact that it would be important in mitigation. For example, most capital defendants are young males, a category of persons tending to be both insecure and boastful about their manliness and sexual prowess. Evidence that they have been the victims of rape and other sexual abuse by male family members and acquaintances deflates those boasts, and capital defendants may resist the introduction of such evidence in a public courtroom. Another example may be their mistreatment during childhood by a beloved family member, one whom they do not want to besmirch or embarrass.

Assuming the defense has navigated its way through those difficult waters, the defense attorney should be ready to put on the case for mitigation. In jurisdictions which authorize two defense attorneys in death penalty cases, it is typical for one attorney to handle the guilt stage and for the other attorney to handle the sentencing stage. This means that the sentencing-stage attorney can focus from the beginning on sentencing issues, working carefully with a "mitigation specialist," essentially an investigator with expertise in digging up facts about the defendant's past that might reflect favorably upon him. Another advantage is that the jury now sees another spokesperson for the defendant, one who has not tried to mislead them into thinking that the defendant didn't actually commit the crime or that he is legally insane. This "new" defense attorney tries to start with a clean slate, working to convince the jury that even though the defendant committed this murder, the best sentencing option would be life in prison and not death.

The defense attorney's goal at the sentencing hearing is to give the jury a picture of the defendant's entire life, working from the constitutionally mandated factor of the character and background of the defendant. *Gregg v. Georgia*, 428 U.S. 153, 96 S.Ct. 2909, 49 L.Ed.2d 859 (1976). At this point in the process, the jury typically will know only about the defendant's worst acts spanning a few moments of his 20+ years of life. Arguing that none of us are as thoroughly evil as our worst solitary acts (or as pure and saintly as our best solitary acts), the defense attorney will ask the jury to consider the defendant's entire life and whether that life should be ended. Evidence presented going to this issue can be a list of good deeds performed at various stages of life, a parade of witnesses recounting their love and admiration for the defendant, and documentation of the defendant's dedicated service to the military, to an employer, and to friends and family in time of need.

Beyond that overall goal, the defense usually will provide whatever evidence can be mustered to establish a few specific mitigating circumstances. Staying with the topic of the defendant's character and background, the defense might focus on evidence that the defendant's mental abilities generally are less than fully normal at the adult level. The evidence might go to establish that the defendant is particularly youthful, borderline mentally retarded, or even mentally ill. Assuming these incapacities were not sufficient to remove the defendant completely from death penalty eligibility, they still can be important mitigating circumstances in the eyes of a death penalty jury.

Moving over to the nature and circumstances of the crime, the defense may try to establish mitigating circumstances of the defendant's mental state at the moment of the murderous acts. This evidence might show that the defendant was under emotional disturbance, duress, or the domination of another at the moment the victim was killed. Some of this evidence may repeat what was found at the previous guilt stage, but now it is being turned in favor of the defendant. While not defenses to the crime, this mens rea evidence can establish mitigating circumstances during the sentencing hearing that serve to avoid the death penalty.

Finally, the Supreme Court has made it clear that the defense can introduce any relevant and material mitigating evidence it wishes to and that the sentencing jury must at least consider that evidence. *Eddings v. Oklahoma*, 455 U.S. 104, 102 S.Ct. 869, 71 L.Ed.2d 1 (1982) and *Lockett v. Ohio*, 438 U.S. 586, 98 S.Ct. 2954, 57 L.Ed.2d 973 (1978). This is in stark contrast to the limitations on the carefully channeled aggravating circumstances that the state can pursue. This "any other" category of mitigating circumstances tends to be the home for wide-ranging evidence about the defendant's unfortunate childhood, his mistreatment by friends, family, and teachers over the years, and his documented good deeds during his life. It also is an opportunity for the defense to play on any residual doubt that any of the individual jurors might have as to whether the defendant committed this crime. Yes, they already have convicted the defendant of murder "beyond a reasonable doubt,'' but some (unreasonable?) doubt might still be lingering in their minds. With more than 125 innocent but wrongly convicted persons released from death row in the current era, one could hardly assume that death penalty juries always get it right. If this defendant is actually innocent, then a life sentence will permit some rectification should the error be discovered. The execution of this defendant makes rectification impossible. The sentencing court, however, need not admit more evidence of the defendant's innocence. *Oregon v. Guzek*, 546 U.S. 517, 126 S.Ct. 1226, 163 L.Ed.2d 1112 (2006).

The prosecuting attorney will have an opportunity to respond to and challenge any and all of the mitigating evidence introduced by the defense. In some instances, such as diminished mental capacity, the state may introduce rebuttal witnesses and other evidence. For other mitigating evidence, such as the defendant having been an eagle scout or a loyal employee, seldom does the prosecution believe it is worthwhile to counter the defense evidence.

Finally, if the defendant is going to testify at any point in all of the legal proceedings in his case, this is that point. While uncommon, the defense attorney may decide that the defendant's personal testimony before the jury as the sentencing hearing is drawing to a close would be beneficial to his case. This may be particularly true if the defendant can and will express remorse for his crimes, sincerely apologize to the victim's family for his actions, and generally put a human face on the jury's decision.

Such capital defendants are rare, though, particularly among typical 19– to 22–year-old convicted murderers, striving mightily to maintain their self-image as tough guys who never apologize and never back down. Emotion, self-doubt, and remorse are simply not parts of their public repertoire, and they truly would rather die than be portrayed as soft and weak. Obviously, to the degree the defendant remains hostile and defiant, this is the last person the defense attorney wants addressing the jury.

Once all of the state's evidence and all of the defense evidence has been presented to the jury at the sentencing hearing, the two attorneys have an opportunity to make their closing arguments to the jury. Which side goes first and whether any rebuttal closing argument is allowed is governed by the individual jurisdictions. The closing argument for the defense to some degree is simply the opposite of that by the prosecution (discussed in § 11.1). In all cases, this is the defense attorney's last opportunity to plead to the jury that the client's life be spared. This plea is based in part upon arguments that specific mitigating circumstances have between proven by the evidence and that they outweigh the aggravating circumstances proven by the state. In addition, given the essentially nonrational decision the jury is being asked to make, the closing argument by the defense pleads also for mercy, for some glint of understanding, for much better treatment than the defendant provided to the victim. The jury's standards for whether or not to take a life are, presumably, more civilized than that of a convicted murderer. Whether they should take a life is to be governed ultimately by what civilized society thinks is right and wrong, not by the standards of the "worst of the worst" murderers.

§ 11.3 Jury Decision

The final, life-or-death decision is now given to the jury. Before they retire to deliberate this heaviest of issues, the jury will once again receive instructions from the trial judge. These instructions will outline, among other things, the aggravating and mitigating circumstances relied upon in this case and the step-by-step procedures the jury must follow from here on out.

For many years in death penalty law, sentencing juries were told simply that their choice was between life in prison or the death penalty. The "death penalty" option was fairly unambiguous, but not so with "life in prison." One recurring political debate is whether "life means life," or whether a prisoner sentenced to life in prison might well be out on parole in a few years. Many states continue to have both possibilities: (1) life in prison without parole (LWOP) and (2) life in prison with parole eligibility in 20 to 30 years. However, for capital murder, the sentence options almost always are limited only to the death penalty and LWOP.

The problem was that juries in death penalty cases didn't know that LWOP was the only alternative to a death sentence. When they would ask the trial judge about this, the judge would not give

them an answer. This uncertainty became a particular problem in death penalty cases in which the
prosecuting attorney's closing argument at the sentencing stage dwelled on the fear that the defendant
would be released to the community and repeat his
horrible crimes unless the jury returned a death
sentence. This has been labeled the "future dangerousness" argument, and it is effective in convincing
juries of their responsibility to protect their community against future violent crimes. Juries in death
penalty cases appear to be concerned mostly about
the defendant's future dangerousness out on the
streets of their community and not so much whether he might be dangerous to other prisoners. Therefore, they want to know if the defendant would ever
be eligible for parole if he is sentenced to life in
prison, or whether they can just lock him up and
throw away the key.

The Supreme Court's major decision on this issue
came in *Simmons v. South Carolina*, 512 U.S. 154,
114 S.Ct. 2187, 129 L.Ed.2d 133 (1994). Even before
jury selection had begun in the *Simmons* case, the
trial judge had granted the prosecutor's motion to
forbid any mention of parole to the jury. In fact, the
defendant in *Simmons* would have been ineligible
for parole if given a life sentence, but the jury never
knew that. The evidence at trial indicated that the
defendant posed a continuing danger of violence to
elderly women, and the prosecutor urged the jury to
return a verdict of death as "an act of self-defense."
The jury even interrupted its final deliberations to
ask the judge specifically if a life sentence carried

the possibility of parole, but the judge refused to answer their question. The *Simmons* jury then returned a sentence of death.

The Supreme Court in *Simmons* held that the defendant's 14th Amendment due process rights were violated by combining the state's repeated "future dangerousness" arguments with the judge's refusal to tell the jury of the defendant's parole ineligibility. Empirical research on this issue over many years has found that a viable LWOP option to the death penalty results in much lower community support for the death penalty, so we can assume that a jury selected from the community would also be influenced by knowing of an LWOP option. The *Simmons* ruling may therefore have an impact on the jury's tendency to return a death sentence, and it must be followed whenever the state broaches the "future dangerousness" argument. This point has been reenforced repeatedly by the Supreme Court, surprisingly in yet more cases coming out of the same jurisdiction. *Kelly v. South Carolina*, 534 U.S. 246, 122 S.Ct. 726, 151 L.Ed.2d 670 (2002); *Shafer v. South Carolina*, 532 U.S. 36, 121 S.Ct. 1263, 149 L.Ed.2d 178 (2001). Also relevant to the jury's choice between death and LWOP, the Supreme Court has held that the trial court must admit evidence of the defendant's good behavior in prison. *Skipper v. South Carolina*, 476 U.S. 1, 106 S.Ct. 1669, 90 L.Ed.2d 1 (1986).

Assuming that the jury now has all of the evidence to which it is entitled and knows what its possible options are, the jury retires to the jury room to deliberate. This is the same room in which this same jury earlier in this same case deliberated and found the defendant guilty of one or more capital crimes. The issue now is not whether he is guilty of a terrible crime but whether he should live or die. The room is private and closed to any and all outside of the members of the jury, in contrast to the very public arena of the rest of the trial process. The role of the jury is to determine which, if any, aggravating circumstances have been proven beyond a reasonable doubt and which, if any, mitigating circumstances have been proven at some lower level of certainty. They then are to weigh the aggravating circumstances against the mitigating circumstances and decide upon a sentence.

Extensive empirical research has been conducted on how death penalty jurors actually make their decisions. The results indicate that the law's determined efforts since *Furman v. Georgia*, 408 U.S. 238, 92 S.Ct. L.Ed.2d 346 (1972) to "guide jury discretion" have had at best mixed results. Death penalty juries in fact tend to confuse aggravating circumstances with mitigating circumstances and commonly stray from those designated in their jury instructions. Juries also confuse the level of certainty they must have in concluding the various aggravating and mitigating circumstances have been proven. Finally, many former members of death penalty juries report that their decision to vote for the death penalty was determined more by their revulsion at viewing the photographs of the victim than by anything the judge or lawyers said in the courtroom. It appears that the judge's instructions to death penalty juries are quite confusing and difficult for lay persons to understand, so the jurors are left largely to their own devices.

If the jurors cannot agree unanimously upon a sentence, they are considered deadlocked and a mistrial is ordered. However, if they do come to agreement, they return to the courtroom and deliver their verdict to those assembled there. Whatever verdict is rendered, the jury's work is done, they are dismissed, and they can finally go home. The members of this jury are not identified publicly and are not subjected to questioning by the press, at least not unless they volunteer to be interviewed. The prosecuting attorney, the defense attorney, and the trial judge all may receive continued, sometimes intense, media coverage based upon their roles in this high profile death penalty case, and they can expect to be involved in other such cases during their careers. However, the most important players in this case, the jurors, fade back into the community from which they came and don't have to even think about the death penalty ever again if they don't want to. It is extremely unlikely that these jurors will ever sit on another death penalty jury, so they can return to the role of spectators, better informed but sobered by their experience.

In most death penalty jurisdictions, including the federal system, the jury verdict is final and the trial judge may not change it. However, some jurisdictions consider the jury verdict to be only advisory, and the trial judge decides upon the final sentence.

It appears that these jurisdictions can continue to permit the judge to opt for LWOP even if the jury's advisory verdict is for death, since this would not violate any of the defendant's constitutional rights. However, the Supreme Court's ruling in *Ring v. Arizona*, 536 U.S. 584, 122 S.Ct. 2428, 153 L.Ed.2d 556 (2002) has made it clear that any final sentence of death must come from a jury and not only the judge, so in essence the judge is not permitted to opt for a death sentence if the jury's verdict is for life.

Assuming that a death sentence is imposed by the jury, the judge and jury disappear into back rooms and the lawyers pack up their briefcases and leave. The defendant is shackled and led from the courtroom, taken for now back to the jail but soon to be driven to his new lodgings on the death row wing of the state's maximum security prison. The friends and family members of the defendant and of the victim undergo emotional releases, stumble through questions from the press, and try to go back to their lives as they were before the trial process began. They often think that the case is finally over and resolved, that the defendant will be executed for his crimes. However, they soon will learn that the case will drag through the courts for years and years, and that it is more likely than not that the condemned offender will never be executed.

PART IV
POST–TRIAL PROCEDURAL ISSUES

CHAPTER 12

APPEALS PROCESS

If sentenced to death, the condemned prisoner is sent to death row in a maximum security prison to await the outcome of appeals and other challenges to the conviction and death sentence. As of the end of 2007, a total of 3,309 such prisoners were housed on the death rows of 35 states and the federal government. These 3,309 death row prisoners constitute one of the largest such populations in the history of the United States and appear to be unrivaled anywhere in the world, now or anytime. These many thousands of condemned murderers on death row tend to take full advantage of all post-trial rights. As a result, a death row prisoner may have been there for 10, 15, or 20 years, slogging through the maze of challenges to his or her sentence.

Any felony conviction and resulting sentence can result in an elaborate and very lengthy process of challenges to that conviction and sentence, but relatively few convicted felons even try to exhaust the possibilities. It is typically the death row inmate and his or her lawyers who can be expected to wring every last drop out of this process. It has two primary stages, the first being direct appeal of the trial-level conviction and sentence, and the second being post-conviction or habeas corpus challenges following direct appeals which were unsuccessful. About two-thirds of them are successful, in that their death sentences are reversed, and they are given either life imprisonment or an entirely new trial and sentencing hearing.

§ 12.1   Courts and Procedures

The appellate model in death penalty cases stems from the Anglo–American common law writ of error. This means that the appellate courts do not simply rehear or retry the case. Instead, the role of our appellate process is to review what happened at trial and to correct errors, if any, made at the trial level that may have affected the outcome. This process often is termed "appellate review," reminding us of the true role played by our appellate courts.

Appellate courts have two primary roles: (1) to correct trial errors and provide justice to the parties, and (2) to declare and, where necessary, to reform the legal doctrine of their jurisdiction. A death row inmate will be interested almost solely in the first role, assuming that such action would reverse either his conviction or his death sentence.

One occasionally hears from a death-sentenced appellant that capital punishment law should be reformed in some way (*e.g.*, to abolish the death penalty for felony-murder). However, one suspects that the immediate goal of removing the appellant from death row may be of more significance to that appellant than achieving sweeping reform of legal doctrine for the general benefit of society in general, unless that reform is the only way to accomplish the desired end. Death row inmates can be expected to raise both kinds of issues on appeal.

All state judicial systems provide at least some opportunity for appellate review. Some states provide only one appellate level, and, in a few states, specialized courts of criminal appeals handle all such cases. Two leading death penalty states, Oklahoma and Texas, are prominent examples. In other death penalty states (*e.g.*, Ohio), all death penalty appeals go directly to the state's general jurisdiction supreme court. In these jurisdictions with only one level of appellate review for death penalty cases, obviously that court must try both to correct trial errors and to make any needed reforms to legal doctrine. However, the primary focus usually is on achieving the correct result in the matter before the court.

Many states provide two levels of appellate review. A death-sentenced appellant first files his appeal in the intermediate court of appeals, which typically is mandated to decide the case. This court of appeals will focus almost solely on reviewing the trial record, correcting any errors found, and deciding whether the magnitude of those errors is so great as to require that either the conviction or the death sentence be overturned. Such an intermediate appellate court is required to follow and enforce the state's legal doctrine as promulgated by the highest court in the state, so fundamental changes in legal doctrine cannot be expected to come from this intermediate appellate court.

If the appellant is unsuccessful at the intermediate appellate court level, he then petitions the state's highest appellate court (typically called the "Supreme Court of [State]"). This is the court of last resort within the jurisdiction, and it has discretion whether or not to hear the case. Given that the intermediate court of appeals is relied upon to correct errors in individual cases, the state supreme court spends most of its time and energy in the second role of appellate courts: declaring and, where necessary, reforming the legal doctrine of its jurisdiction.

Most fundamental, each state has its own state constitution, and the state's highest court is the final arbiter of what is and is not acceptable under that state constitution. Obviously, all courts, state and federal, are bound by interpretations of the United States Constitution as rendered by the United States Supreme Court. However, in death penalty cases, those federal interpretations provide only a floor beneath which the states may not go. An individual state may provide a higher floor for its own specific state death penalty system through interpretation of its own state constitution. For example, prior to the United States Supreme Court decision in *Roper v. Simmons*, 543 U.S. 551, 125 S.Ct. 1183, 161 L.Ed.2d 1 (2005), the Court had interpreted the United States Constitution to require a minimum age of 16 for imposition of the death penalty (*Thompson v. Oklahoma*, 487 U.S. 815, 108 S.Ct. 2687, 101 L.Ed.2d 702 (1988)) but had rejected any federal requirement of a minimum age of 17 or 18 (*Stanford v. Kentucky*, 492 U.S. 361, 109 S.Ct. 2969, 106 L.Ed.2d 306 (1989)). Nonetheless, the Florida Supreme Court interpreted the Florida Constitution to require a minimum age of 17 for the death penalty in Florida. *Brennan v. State*, 754 So.2d 1 (Fla.1999). Such a fundamental interpretation of a state's legal doctrine would normally come only from that state's highest appellate court.

The United States Constitution has never been interpreted to guarantee a constitutional right to any appellate review of a criminal conviction or sentence. In capital cases specifically, however, the Supreme Court has commented favorably on appellate review being mandated by a state's death penalty statute. *Gregg v. Georgia*, 428 U.S. 153, 96 S.Ct. 2909, 49 L.Ed.2d 859 (1976). The constitutional issue need not be faced, since all jurisdictions (state and federal) now guarantee review by at least one level of appellate courts, often termed an ''appeal as of right.'' Although an ''appeal as of right'' may not be mandated by the United States Constitution, nonetheless certain constitutional protections do attach once a jurisdiction has granted such a right to appeal for criminal defendants.

For example, the 14th Amendment guarantees that a free transcript of the trial record must be provided to indigent criminal defendants so that they can obtain appellate review. *Griffin v. Illinois*, 351 U.S. 12, 76 S.Ct. 585, 100 L.Ed. 891 (1956). Similarly, if the state guarantees criminal defendants a right to an appeal, then indigent defendants must be provided with a free (state-paid) appellate attorney to represent the defendant during that appeal as of right. *Douglas v. California*, 372 U.S. 353, 83 S.Ct. 814, 9 L.Ed.2d 811 (1963). This constitutional right to appointed counsel does not extend past this point, into either the discretionary appellate review or the subsequent state post conviction challenges. *Ross v. Moffitt*, 417 U.S. 600, 94 S.Ct. 2437, 41 L.Ed.2d 341 (1974); *Murray v. Giarratano*, 492 U.S. 1, 109 S.Ct. 2765, 106 L.Ed.2d 1 (1989). *Barbour v. Allen*, ___ U.S. ___, 127 S.Ct. 2996, 168 L.Ed.2d 707 (2007) (cert. denied). Coming at this issue from the other direction, no constitutional provision prohibits a death row prisoner from making a knowing and intelligent waiver of this right to appeal and, in such cases, the state then has no obligation to pursue appellate review despite the defendant's wishes. *Gilmore v. Utah*, 429 U.S. 1012, 97 S.Ct. 436, 50 L.Ed.2d 632 (1976).

Assume that the convicted capital defendant, now sitting on death row, has an appellate attorney, almost undoubtedly one appointed by the court under the requirement of *Douglas*. In many jurisdictions, this appellate attorney is another lawyer in the public defender's office, albeit in the appellate division of that office. This attorney's task is to review the trial record in detail, highlight any and all errors made at that level, and brief the case thoroughly, raising every reasonable legal challenge and exposing every perceived error made at trial. Even if the appointed appellate counsel decides that there is nothing worth appealing, that appellate counsel nonetheless must file a brief with the appellate court that refers to anything in the trial record "that might arguably support an appeal." *Anders v. California*, 386 U.S. 738, 87 S.Ct. 1396, 18 L.Ed.2d 493 (1967). Either way, unless the defendant refuses to appeal altogether, the appellate court receives a brief from the appellant-defendant. The respondent-state will then file its brief, typically refuting the appellant's claims and assertions. According to the rules of the specific state, the parties may also make oral arguments before the court, and then the court begins working to decide the case.

In most jurisdictions, appellate review of death penalty cases is given priority over both noncapital criminal appeals and civil appeals. However, many appellate courts have very heavy caseloads to wade through, and capital cases in particular (the only literally "life or death" cases) usually receive enormous attention to detail. As a result, decisions in these cases can be many months or even years in coming. Meanwhile, the condemned prisoner sits on death row in the state's maximum security prison, wondering daily when the next shoe will drop. The inmate's lawyer can do little if anything on behalf of the client until the court makes its decision, and the appellate attorney for the state (typically a lawyer in the state attorney general's office) is similarly off the case for now. The entire case is dead in the water until the appellate court issues its decision.

The case comes back to life when the intermediate appellate court issues its decision. If the conviction and/or death sentence is reversed, the case may go back to the trial court to start over again. However, usually the state can appeal this reversal to the state supreme court, seeking in essence a reversal of the reversal. If appellant-defendant loses at this round of the appellate process, almost always that defendant will want to take the case to the next level. However, the first step in this stage of the process is to petition for discretionary review, and the death row inmate may no longer have a lawyer to assist him in preparing this petition. In many jurisdictions, the state supreme court does not have to hear the case but may do so if it chooses. Given the major importance of death penalty cases, they do tend to get picked for discretionary review, certainly more often than other kinds of cases. Pretty much the same routine will be followed as in the first appellate review, with briefs being filed and oral argument being made by the respective attorneys. The state supreme court then spends as much time as it needs to decide the case, ranging from months to years in some instances. Assuming the state supreme court denies relief to the petitioner, the case can be taken directly to the United States Supreme Court, but the chances of the Supreme Court agreeing to hear the case at this juncture are less than 1%.

If all appellate options are exhausted, there exists a fundamental assumption that the case has reached an end. Indeed, the Supreme Court has held that "direct appeal is the primary avenue for review of a conviction or sentence, and death penalty cases are no exception. When the process of direct review . . . comes to an end, a presumption of finality and legality attaches to the conviction and sentence." *Barefoot v. Estelle*, 463 U.S. 880, 103 S.Ct. 3383, 77 L.Ed.2d 1090 (1983). Despite the implications of this language from *Barefoot*, appellate review of death penalty cases is rarely if ever the end of the case in our courts. It can be expected to take on a new life under a new name as it transforms into post-conviction challenges in state and federal courts (see chapter 13).

§ 12.2 Issues

Appellate review of a death penalty case almost always will examine both stages of the trial process: conviction and sentencing. The substance and procedures involved in finding a defendant guilty of a capital crime at trial are essentially the same as for noncapital cases, so appellate review of the conviction process proceeds in the same manner. A reversal of the conviction is the appellant-defendant's first choice and the state's most feared outcome, because the death sentence falls also if the conviction is reversed. The entire case is knocked out, and the state must begin again from square one if it wishes to put this defendant in prison or on death row. This means a completely new guilt stage and sentencing stage within the trial process, a long, labor-intensive, and expensive activity for everyone concerned (see chapters 9, 10, and 11). Therefore, even in cases in which little error can reasonably be attributed to the guilt stage of the trial process, death row inmates can be expected to challenge their convictions as strongly as possible, and the state can be expected to oppose this specific challenge with equal aggressiveness.

The other major trial court conclusion challenged on appeal is the imposition of a sentence of death upon the appellant-defendant. This is very much a second choice for the defense, since the original conviction of murder still stands. The only prize won by such a victory is either another sentencing hearing (see chapters 9 and 11) or a reduction of the death sentence by the appellate court to a sentence of life in prison without parole. Appellate review of the sentencing stage of the trial process in a death penalty case is unique, unparalleled by anything else the appellate court does. It is difficult enough for an appellate court, far removed from the trial both in time and distance, to recapture an accurate sense of the defendant, lawyers, judge, or witnesses, even as it tries to reconstruct factual determinations. The sentencing decision combines factual determinations with the emotional and moral conclusions bound up in the trial environment.

For an appellate court to determine whether a death sentencing decision was accurate and appropriate is a daunting undertaking indeed.

Within the broad appellate categories of conviction challenges and sentencing challenges, death penalty appeals may raise three specific kinds of issues. The first issue raises claims in substantive criminal law. Such claims by the appellant-defendant might frame questions as to the adequacy of proof of each and every element of the crime for which he was convicted. Since capital crimes in the current era are all murder cases, this means that the defendant is challenging one or more of the elements of murderous intent and/or the acts of murder. Other substantive law issues can include special defenses such as insanity.

The second general kind of issues typically raised on appeal are in the area of criminal procedure. The most common issue in death penalty appeals, for instance, is whether the defense attorney at trial provided "ineffective assistance of counsel" to the appellant-defendant. The 6th Amendment guarantees a criminal defendant the "assistance of counsel for his defense," and death row prisoners commonly believe that their trial lawyer performed so poorly that their 6th Amendment right was violated (see chapter 15). *Strickland v. Washington*, 466 U.S. 668, 104 S.Ct. 2052, 80 L.Ed.2d 674 (1984). Other criminal procedure issues in capital cases are the same garden variety of issues seen in almost all noncapital criminal appeals: search and seizure, confessions, and imposition of the exclusionary rule.

The standards in each of these areas are no higher for capital cases than for noncapital cases, but they may get more attention here simply because capital cases are pursued so aggressively on appeal and later.

The third kind of specific issues involves an assortment of systemic challenges. These issues appeared to have nothing to do with the appellant-defendant's specific conviction and death sentence, but they impact him only as a member of a class. For example, such issues might challenge the death penalty for the mentally retarded or for juvenile offenders, or challenge the death penalty for non-homicidal rape of a child. *Atkins v. Virginia*, 536 U.S. 304, 122 S.Ct. 2242, 153 L.Ed.2d 335 (2002); *Roper v. Simmons*, 543 U.S. 551, 125 S.Ct. 1183, 161 L.Ed.2d 1 (2005); *Kennedy v. Louisiana*, ___ U.S. ___, 128 S.Ct. 2641, 171 L.Ed.2d 525 (2008). Assuming the defendant is a member of the class so identified, a ruling excluding the entire class from the death penalty would incidentally exclude the defendant as well. These systemic challenges are almost never considered on first impression by an intermediate appellate court, but the court of last resort (typically the state supreme court) may consider such challenges, particularly when made under that state's constitution.

§ 12.3   Results

By bringing these appeals, the appellant-defendant is seeking, if not absolute vindication, at least a reversal of his conviction and/or death sentence.

The appellee-state in contrast, wants to avoid if at all possible having to redo this case. Even a casual reading of chapters 9, 10, and 11 provides a sense of just how much time, energy, and money is invested in bringing a capital case from the original charge through a death verdict. Sending the case back to the trial level, often after many years have passed, witnesses have died or moved away, and physical evidence is nowhere to be found, means either that the case must be plea bargained to a prison sentence or retried under very difficult circumstances. The judiciary, while officially neutral, is acutely aware of the huge burden that capital cases place on state trial and appellate courts. It is apparent that appellate judges aggressively seek ways to avoid having to do such a case more than once. Therefore, it may be said that the only party to an appeal who wants a reversal is the appellant-defendant and his lawyer.

If the appellate courts reverse the appellant-defendant's conviction of the capital crime, then he is now back to being an "accused" and in his original pre-trial status. If the state wishes to convict the accused of a capital crime and see him sentenced to death, then the entire trial process must be completed once again: jury selection, guilt stage, and sentencing stage. For the state's prosecuting attorneys to be able to navigate that challenging course yet one more time is anything but certain, so often the state is more interested in a plea bargain at this point than they were originally.

It is somewhat simpler if the appellate courts reverse only the death sentence and affirm the conviction. Nonetheless, a new jury must still be selected, given that the factors upon which a death sentence is to be based must be found by a jury and not just by a judge. *Ring v. Arizona*, 536 U.S. 584, 122 S.Ct. 2428, 153 L.Ed.2d 556 (2002). The guilt stage need not be repeated, since the defendant's original conviction of a capital crime remains valid, and the case can move directly from the selection of the jury to the sentencing stage of the trial process. However, this is a new jury, completely unfamiliar with the facts of the case, so the state will have a much greater burden to present evidence and argument than would have been necessary if this was the original jury that had sat through and decided the original guilt stage.

Given the extraordinary complexity of death penalty guilt stages and sentencing stages, implemented through the imperfection of human actors, an error-free death penalty trial may well be nearly impossible. On appeal, the question is not whether errors were made at trial but whether those errors were "harmless errors" and thus do not require a reversal of either the conviction or the death sentence. Errors having their source in violations of constitutional rights are considered to be more serious and less likely to be harmless errors than those errors not grounded in constitutional rights. One continuing theme that supports findings of harmless error is whether the rest of the nonerroneous evidence indicates that the jury reached the right decision regardless of the error. If the case "came out right" even though errors were made, it makes little sense to appellate courts to send the case back to the trial level to do over. However, a constitutional error will not be considered harmless unless the appellate court finds beyond a reasonable doubt that the error did not contribute to the jury's verdict. *Chapman v. California*, 386 U.S. 18, 87 S.Ct. 824, 17 L.Ed.2d 705 (1967). Some constitutional errors are not just routine trial errors but are "structural defects in the constitution of the trial mechanism" requiring automatic reversal. *Arizona v. Fulminante*, 499 U.S. 279, 111 S.Ct. 1246, 113 L.Ed.2d 302 (1991).

A repeating issue coming before the Supreme Court has been what to do when an appellate court finds one of the aggravating circumstances to be invalid but other aggravating factors to be fully acceptable. It is the trial jury's primary task to evaluate such aggravating circumstances and to weigh them against any mitigating circumstances, so the first thought might be to reverse the death sentence and refer it back to the trial level for a new sentencing hearing. However, as indicated above, this would require selection of a new jury and an extended sentencing stage, which is a very high price for the prosecuting attorneys and judiciary to pay. Therefore, the Supreme Court has tried to find ways to approve of the appellate courts reweighing the remaining valid aggravating and mitigating circumstances and coming to a conclusion as to the appellant-defendant's sentence. The original trial jury would already have found all of these remaining valid aggravating circumstances, so this would appear to meet the requirements of *Ring v. Arizona*, 536 U.S. 584, 122 S.Ct. 2428, 153 L.Ed.2d 556 (2002).

One of the early cases in the current death penalty era to examine this issue was *Barclay v. Florida*, 463 U.S. 939, 103 S.Ct. 3418, 77 L.Ed.2d 1134 (1983). This was a pre-*Ring* case in which the trial judge made findings as to aggravating circumstances and then sentenced the defendant to death despite a jury recommendation of life imprisonment. In *Barclay*, the Florida Supreme Court found that one of the trial judge's aggravating circumstances was not authorized by the Florida statute, so they threw it out and then re-evaluated the remaining aggravating circumstances found by the trial judge (no mitigating circumstances had been found). The Florida Supreme Court thereby upheld the appellant-defendant's death sentence without sending it back for a new sentencing hearing before a trial judge and jury. The Supreme Court in *Barclay* approved of this process of affirming a death sentence after trial-level errors had been found and corrected.

Within a few years, two death penalty cases came out of Mississippi which clarified this issue. In the first case, the trial jury had not been instructed properly on the required level of criminal intent for the death penalty under *Enmund v. Florida*, 458 U.S. 782, 102 S.Ct. 3368, 73 L.Ed.2d 1140 (1982) before returning a death verdict. *Cabana v. Bullock*,

474 U.S. 376, 106 S.Ct. 689, 88 L.Ed.2d 704 (1986). The state appellate courts in *Bullock* had not addressed this criminal intent issue, so the Supreme Court vacated the death sentence and remanded the case for a factual finding as to criminal intent, followed by a sentencing decision. However, the Supreme Court in *Bullock* noted that this new finding and resulting sentencing can be conducted by any "appropriate tribunal—be it an appellate court, a trial judge, or a jury."

A few years later, the Supreme Court decided *Clemons v. Mississippi*, 494 U.S. 738, 110 S.Ct. 1441, 108 L.Ed.2d 725 (1990). There the jury had found two aggravating circumstances, one of which was the constitutionally invalid factor that the crime was "especially heinous, atrocious, or cruel" and the other of which was the acceptable factor of the murder occurring during a robbery. The Mississippi Supreme Court had reviewed and affirmed the death sentence after throwing out the unacceptable aggravating circumstance, all without ever remanding the case for a jury determination. In *Clemons*, the Supreme Court held that, among other things, the constitution permits state appellate courts to engage in reweighing or harmless-error analyses when errors have occurred in the sentencing stage of the trial process and the appellate court has struck an aggravating circumstance. This issue was expressly not addressed in *Ring*, so *Clemons* continues to be good law. In its latest ruling, the Supreme Court held that a death sentence can be upheld if another valid sentencing factor compensates for the invalid sentencing factor. *Brown v. Sanders*, 546 U.S. 212, 126 S.Ct. 884, 163 L.Ed.2d 723 (2006).

The *Clemons* rule may provide appellate courts the best of both worlds. Those courts are relatively free to identify and correct errors on appeals without the cost to the state and to the judiciary being a new guilt stage and/or sentencing stage of the trial process. However, the downside may be that a key part of the jury's role in death penalty cases is diminished when appellate courts perform the re-sentencing function after errors are found in the original sentencing process.

CHAPTER 13

POST–CONVICTION CHALLENGES

The direct appeals process now being over, the death row inmate can and almost always will begin to attack his conviction and death sentence through collateral proceedings. Appellate review is seen as a continuation of the original criminal proceeding (*State of Wherever v. John Doe*), but the collateral attack or habeas corpus proceedings are seen as a civil lawsuit challenging the legality of the prisoner's criminal conviction and sentence. It typically will be labeled as the petitioner versus the prison warden or state director of corrections (*John Doe v. Sarah Smith, Director of Corrections, State of Wherever*). These post-conviction challenges typically begin first in state courts and then move to the federal courts, often raising the same or similar issues as were raised at trial and during the direct appeals process.

§ 13.1 Courts and Procedures

Various forms of state collateral proceedings can be found among the death penalty states, allowing the death row prisoner yet another opportunity to challenge his conviction and death sentence in the state courts. However, the Supreme Court has made it clear that these state collateral proceedings are not constitutionally required as an adjunct to or extension of the preceding state criminal trial and appellate process. *Murray v. Giarratano*, 492 U.S. 1, 109 S.Ct. 2765, 106 L.Ed.2d 1 (1989). Nonetheless, state collateral proceedings are a central part of the overall post-trial review process for death row prisoners.

Commonly, the first step is for the petitioner-defendant to file a state-level post-conviction challenge in that state's trial-level court, located typically in the county in which the death row inmate is now imprisoned. Although this is a trial-level court, these collateral challenges are presented solely to the judge with no jury involved. This collateral attack will take the form of a civil lawsuit, pitting the death row inmate against the prison warden and/or the state director of corrections and suing for release from prison. At the outset, at least, the death row prisoner will be on his own in this endeavor, in that there is no constitutional right to appointed counsel in such cases, even though many states will appoint counsel under statutory provisions. *Murray v. Giarratano*, 492 U.S. 1, 109 S.Ct. 2765, 106 L.Ed.2d 1 (1989). Unlike the appellate courts, habeas courts are not limited to issues raised at trial but typically may undertake independent fact-finding if warranted. State-level collateral relief proceedings typically empower the trial-level judge to hold a hearing to gather any further evidence deemed necessary to make a judgment about the legality of the petitioner-defendant's conviction and death sentence. *Townsend v. Sain*, 372 U.S. 293, 83 S.Ct. 745, 9 L.Ed.2d 770 (1963).

If the death-sentenced petitioner loses at this first level of the state collateral proceeding, then the case begins to work its way back up through the state appellate process, this time as a collateral attack instead of as a criminal appeal. The state appellate courts may be asked to rule on essentially the same issues they considered during the previous appellate process, but the collateral process can also be expected to raise issues not a part of the former appellate case. In any event, the appeal of the collateral case typically will be considered by an intermediate state appellate court, and/or a specialized state court of criminal appeals, and/or the state supreme court. For these courts, this will be the second time they have seen this case, the first having been on direct appeal. The same process of written briefs and oral arguments applies, and the case can take years to make its way through the various levels of state collateral attack. In fact, it is typical for state collateral proceedings to not have time line requirements as strict as those found in the appellate process. As before, the final step would be to ask the United States Supreme Court to hear the case, but again this has about a 1% chance of being successful.

If the state death row inmate has lost at trial, lost through the state direct appeals process, and lost through state collateral attack, then that death row prisoner can be expected to turn to the federal habeas corpus process. The federal habeas process usually does not and cannot start until all of the state processes have been completed. This is a new, federal lawsuit, although often raising almost all of the same issues raised in the state collateral attack proceeding. It is filed originally in a federal district (trial level) court located in the same geographical area as the state's death row prison. In essence, such cases assert that a state is depriving the petitioner-defendant of the rights to "life, liberty, and property" that are guaranteed by the United States Constitution and other federal laws. 28 U.S.C. § 2241, *et seq.* Thus, a federal district court reviews the state trial proceedings and may have a fact-finding hearing if deemed necessary. After presenting the case to this federal judge, the death row inmate, the defense attorneys, and the state's attorneys sit back and wait for a ruling by the federal district judge.

Assuming the petitioner-defendant loses in the federal habeas action at the district court level, he can be expected to appeal that decision to the federal circuit court of appeals for that geographical circuit. Again, written briefs are filed and oral arguments are made, and then the circuit court retires to decide the case sometime in the months or years to come. If the death row inmate loses at this level, he has one more opportunity to petition the United States Supreme Court to agree to hear the case. While the chances of the Supreme Court hearing the case at this juncture may be slightly greater than before, the probability is still very slight.

After the inmate has taken the case through the federal habeas process once, there will be very little opportunity to bring issues back to the federal courts. Habeas petitions originally were conceived as independent civil lawsuits, so multiple suits could raise the same or similar issues without much restriction. However, modern statutory limitations on federal habeas almost totally preclude a second or subsequent habeas petition. 28 U.S.C. §§ 2244, 2253, 2254. The "successive petition doctrine" generally prohibits subsequent petitions that raise claims already adjudicated in the first petition. The "abuse of writ doctrine" precludes the petitioner-defendant from raising claims in a subsequent petition that were not raised in the first petition. With very few narrow exceptions, this means that the death row inmate must raise any and all issues in his first federal habeas petition, and the habeas courts will consider and decide those issues once and only once.

Now, typically at least eight to ten years after being sentenced to death, the condemned murderer has exhausted the obvious court challenges. To be sure, his attorneys can be expected to continue to seek court relief in a variety of other peripheral challenges, but the major line of appellate and collateral attack cases are over and almost always cannot be revived. *Herrera v. Collins*, 506 U.S. 390, 113 S.Ct. 853, 122 L.Ed.2d 203 (1993); *House v. Bell*, 547 U.S. 518, 126 S.Ct. 2064, 165 L.Ed.2d 1 (2006). Following this complete exhaustion of all court challenges to the conviction and to the death sentence, the only hope left for the death row prisoner is to receive clemency from the state governor (see chapter 14).

§ 13.2 Issues

What issues and claims can be considered in federal habeas petitions? First of all, since its creation, federal habeas corpus has required the petitioner to prove that he is being detained "in violation of the Constitution or laws or treaties of the United States." These are federal cases in federal courts claiming violations of the federal constitution. Violations of state law, therefore, no matter how egregious, are simply irrelevant in federal habeas proceedings. Of course, state death row prisoners will already have taken their cases through state trials, state appellate reviews, and state collateral proceedings, so claims of state law violations should have been aired at least three times. In death penalty cases, almost all claims in federal habeas proceedings are based on constitutional provisions and not upon other federal law.

One of the most extreme cases underlining the requirement of a federal constitutional issue in federal habeas proceedings is *Herrera v. Collins*, 506 U.S. 390, 113 S.Ct. 853, 122 L.Ed.2d 203 (1993). In *Herrera*, the petitioner had discovered new evidence strongly suggesting that he was in fact innocent and wrongly convicted years before at his state trial. However, the Supreme Court held that claims of actual innocence based upon newly discovered evidence do not state grounds for federal habeas relief unless they also show a violation of the federal constitution during the previous state criminal proceedings. Chief Justice Rehnquist's majority opinion in *Herrera* did "assume, for the sake of argument in deciding this case, that in a capital case a truly persuasive demonstration of 'actual innocence' made after trial would render the execution of a defendant unconstitutional." However, the "threshold showing for such an assumed right" would be "extraordinarily high," and the petitioner in *Herrera* fell short of that threshold. Justice Blackmun's dissent saw things a little differently, finding several constitutional violations in *Herrera* and observing that "[t]he execution of a person who can show that he is innocent comes perilously close to simple murder." Only four months after the Supreme Court decided *Herrera*, the State of Texas executed Lionel Herrera, who maintained his innocence until the end.

In *House v. Bell*, 547 U.S. 518, 126 S.Ct. 2064, 165 L.Ed.2d 1 (2006), the petitioner had been on death row for 20 years, but new DNA evidence raised strong questions as to whether he was actually the person who had raped and murdered his neighbor. An inmate's claims normally would be procedurally barred in a case so old, but the Supreme Court thought that this new evidence was more likely than not to raise reasonable doubts in the minds of jurors. Therefore, the Court ordered that Bell can challenge his conviction and death sentence with his newly-found new evidence.

Although federal habeas cases must be based upon violations of federal constitutional law, not all constitutional provisions will be considered. The Supreme Court has particularly been unreceptive to providing federal habeas relief based on 4th Amendment search and seizure issues. *Stone v. Powell*, 428 U.S. 465, 96 S.Ct. 3037, 49 L.Ed.2d 1067 (1976). In *Powell*, the Supreme Court noted that the state prisoner seeking review of his 4th Amendment issue in federal habeas proceedings had already had full and fair litigation of his 4th Amendment claim in state courts. In such cases, *Powell* prohibits relief, in large part because the Supreme Court is disenchanted generally with the exclusionary rule which suppresses evidence seized in violation of the 4th Amendment and found insufficient justification to extend review of such cases to federal habeas jurisdiction.

The Supreme Court in *Powell* seemed willing to extend this notion to other types of constitutional violations as well, but this has not happened. Claims based upon 5th Amendment issues of improper admissions of confessions are still reviewable in federal habeas. *Withrow v. Williams*, 507 U.S. 680, 113 S.Ct. 1745, 123 L.Ed.2d 407 (1993). Similarly, federal habeas courts continue to examine claims of ineffective assistance of counsel under the 6th Amendment. *Kimmelman v. Morrison*, 477 U.S. 365, 106 S.Ct. 2574, 91 L.Ed.2d 305 (1986). More general claims of denial of due process or equal protection also continue to be reviewable in federal habeas. *Jackson v. Virginia*, 443 U.S. 307, 99 S.Ct.

2781, 61 L.Ed.2d 560 (1979); *Rose v. Mitchell*, 443 U.S. 545, 99 S.Ct. 2993, 61 L.Ed.2d 739 (1979).

§ 13.3   Results

As described earlier, the result the petitioner-defendant wants is a reversal of his conviction of a capital crime or, failing that, a reversal of his death sentence. If only his death sentence is reversed, the petitioner typically would prefer to receive a life sentence directly from the federal habeas court. If, instead, the case is remanded for a new sentencing hearing, the defendant once again faces the Hobson's choice of either a death sentence or life imprisonment. Whatever the outcome, the state almost always wants a result exactly the opposite of that sought by the petitioner-defendant.

Suppose the petitioner-defendant "wins" the federal habeas case by getting the Supreme Court to agree that the conviction or death sentence would not stand under current law. This may be a hollow victory, because the Supreme Court has held that the constitutionality of a prisoner's detention is to be determined not by current law but by the law as it existed at the time the conviction became final. *Teague v. Lane*, 489 U.S. 288, 109 S.Ct. 1060, 103 L.Ed.2d 334 (1989). Under *Teague*, federal habeas relief may not be granted based on a retroactive application of a new constitutional rule established by a Supreme Court case decided after the petitioner's conviction. Even more sweeping, *Teague* prohibits federal courts from declaring new constitutional law rules in federal habeas cases. *Teague* interprets federal habeas corpus law to ensure that state convictions comply with the federal law existing at the time of the conviction and not as a vehicle for continuing reexamination of final judgments based upon subsequent changes in legal doctrine. *Sawyer v. Smith*, 497 U.S. 227, 110 S.Ct. 2822, 111 L.Ed.2d 193 (1990).

Two narrow exceptions to *Teague* exist, according to *Saffle v. Parks*, 494 U.S. 484, 110 S.Ct. 1257, 108 L.Ed.2d 415 (1990). First, the habeas petitioner in the instant case can benefit from a new constitutional rule if that new rule makes his conduct no longer criminal or prohibits the death penalty in cases such as this. An example might be a juvenile or mentally retarded offender seeking federal habeas relief from the death penalty after the Supreme Court has held that the death penalty for such offenders violates the 8th and 14th Amendments. *Roper v. Simmons*, 543 U.S. 551, 125 S.Ct. 1183, 161 L.Ed.2d 1 (2005); *Atkins v. Virginia*, 536 U.S. 304, 122 S.Ct. 2242, 153 L.Ed.2d 335 (2002). Obviously, these kinds of cases are few and far between, but they do occur.

The second narrow exception to *Teague* applies to "watershed rules of criminal procedure" that are necessary to the fundamental fairness of the criminal proceeding and "without which the likelihood of an accurate conviction is seriously diminished." This is a very severe test, in that such rules must go far beyond just aiming to improve the accuracy of the criminal trial process but also must "alter our understanding of the bedrock procedural elements."

The Supreme Court in *Teague* noted in passing that such exceptions will be rare, because it is "unlikely that many such components of basic due process have yet to emerge." It may be just a little short-sighted to announce that additional "components of basic due process" are unlikely to emerge, certainly with death penalty law continuing to be governed by "evolving standards of decency that mark the progress of a maturing society." Nonetheless, it is certainly true that the rapid discovery of such basic due process components which so characterized the Warren Court of the 1960s did not continue during the Burger Court, the Rehnquist Court, or the Roberts Court.

The results, therefore, of post-conviction challenges to a conviction of a capital crime and/or to a sentence of death can take several forms. The death row prisoner can prevail, see the conviction and/or death sentence reversed, and prepare to begin all over again at the trial level. The death row prisoner can lose, see the conviction and death sentence affirmed yet one more time by the courts, and prepare to seek clemency and, if unsuccessful there, to face execution. The third, in-between possible result is to be found to be correct on the current law but precluded from relief by *Teague v. Lane*, 489 U.S. 288, 109 S.Ct. 1060, 103 L.Ed.2d 334 (1989). In these strange, never never land cases, the death row prisoner also prepares to seek clemency and, if unsuccessful there, to face execution.

CHAPTER 14

CLEMENCY AND EXECUTION PROCEEDINGS

About two-thirds of death sentences imposed at the trial level are reversed either on direct appeal or during collateral proceedings, a gauntlet of inspection by four to six courts over a period of perhaps ten years or more. However, for that one-third of death sentences which survive this gauntlet, the final effort to avoid the actual imposition of that death sentence will be to plead the case before the state governor or, if it is a federal death sentence, before the United States President. The truly "legal" challenges to a death sentence occur only in the courts, both trial and appellate, and the clemency petition to the governor is essentially a plea for mercy despite having had all of the court rulings go the other way. If clemency petitions fail, the last stage of the death penalty process is the execution of the condemned murderer. Such executions are carefully choreographed and controlled by the prison authorities and are more akin to routine hospital procedures than to the public hangings and beheadings in former death penalty eras.

§ 14.1 Clemency Procedures and Standards

The concept of clemency is both very old and very broad. It is sought from the chief executive of the jurisdiction in which the convicted offender is being imprisoned, either the governor in a state case or the president in a federal case. Executive clemency encompasses a wide range of options, including pardons, amnesties, reprieves, and commutations. A pardon is the most sweeping, in that it absolves a specific offender of responsibility for the offense. Rarely if ever would a death row inmate in the current death penalty era seek or receive a pardon for his offense. Amnesties usually are sought by and granted to groups of individuals, such as delinquent tax payers or war resisters. As with pardons, amnesties are not in the cards for death row inmates. Reprieves provide only short term, temporary relief. For example, a governor might issue a reprieve suspending a scheduled execution for 30 days pending further consideration of a final decision. Finally, and most significant for this discussion, commutations neither excuse the offense, forgive the offender, nor delay the execution. A commutation is a grant of mercy, generally substituting a lesser punishment for the greater punishment currently imposed upon the petitioner. A commutation is the goal of the death row prisoner, hoping for a replacement of the death sentence with some form of a prison sentence. The most common form of relief would be for the governor to commute the offender's death sentence to life imprisonment without parole.

In comparison to the strict and complex legal procedures that dominate court-based procedures of direct appeals and collateral challenges, the required procedures in clemency requests seem like another world. The death row inmate's continuing quest has now shifted in locale from the judicial branch of government to the executive branch, with an accompanying change from legal arguments and a focus on the narrow rules of procedure to political policy arguments and a focus on public opinion polls and hopes for reelection. Clemency is still pursued typically by a defense attorney and opposed by a state's attorney, but the difference in forum from courts and judges to administrative boards and governors requires that these two opposing counsel act less like legal advocates and more like political lobbyists.

The most common clemency process requires that the death row inmate's lawyers file the clemency petition with a state board (typically appointed by the governor), often the same board that handles parole petitions from prisoners serving life sentences. This board reviews the written petition and also may hear oral testimony from the attorneys on both sides, from members of the victim's family, from members of the offender's family, and perhaps from political action groups. The board's final action is to send a recommendation to the governor which usually is advisory but which, in states such as Texas, may bind the governor's hands in considering a grant of clemency. State governors commonly wait until almost the last day in deciding whether to grant clemency to a death row inmate scheduled for execution. If the governor grants clemency, typically the offender's death sentence is changed to life in prison without parole. If the governor does not grant clemency, then execution is imminent.

The Supreme Court has seldom ventured into clemency issues, but the Court's early observation was that clemency is "an act of grace ... It is the private, though official, act of the executive magistrate." *United States v. Wilson*, 32 U.S. (7 Pet.) 150, 8 L.Ed. 640 (1833). Probably the most significant case during the current death penalty era is *Ohio Adult Parole Authority v. Woodard*, 523 U.S. 272, 118 S.Ct. 1244, 140 L.Ed.2d 387 (1998). In *Woodard*, the Supreme Court reaffirmed the long-standing principle that executive pardons and commutations "are rarely, if ever, appropriate subjects for judicial review." *Woodard* reminds us that 14th Amendment due process is not violated by committing the clemency power to the authority of the state governor. The Ohio procedure being challenged required the parole authority to conduct a clemency hearing within 45 days of the scheduled execution, complete a clemency review, and make a recommendation to the governor. The Supreme Court in *Woodard* held that neither the 14th Amendment due process clause nor the 5th Amendment privilege against self-incrimination are violated by such a clemency proceeding. At this stage of the process, the "defendant in effect accepts the finality of the death sentence for purposes of adjudication, and appeals for clemency as a matter of grace."

Woodard characterized the granting of executive clemency as "a matter of grace, thus allowing the executive to consider a wide range of factors not comprehended by earlier judicial proceedings and sentencing determinations." To be a bit more candid clemency decisions are intensely political decisions, being made by political leaders beholden to the voting public for their present jobs and often hoping to return to that voting public either for reelection to that same office or for election to a new office. Mercy and justice undoubtedly are part of their consideration, and these are the points most likely to be stressed in the governor's public comments about clemency for a death row prisoner. However, in the real world, behind-the-scenes discussions and decisions about individual requests for clemency, mercy and justice concerns are overwhelmed by political considerations.

Nonetheless, clemency continues to be seen as the last chance to correct errors. The Supreme Court in *Herrera v. Collins*, 506 U.S. 390, 113 S.Ct. 853, 122 L.Ed.2d 203 (1993) noted in passing that clemency "is deeply rooted in our Anglo–American tradition of law, and is the historic remedy for preventing miscarriages of justice where judicial process has been exhausted." *Herrera* characterized executive clemency as "the 'fail safe' in our criminal justice system" and observed that "history is replete with examples of wrongfully convicted persons who have been pardoned in the wake of after-discovered evidence establishing their innocence.''

As of the end of the year 2007, about 8,000 persons had received death sentences in the current death penalty era. From these 7,500 death sentences had come 1,099 executions (14% of all sentences) and about 240 grants of clemency (3% of all sentences). Keeping in mind the undercurrent of strong but unspoken political considerations, the official reasons given for these grants of clemency have been (1) lingering doubt about the condemned person's guilt, (2) reduced blameworthiness from mental problems, and (3) disproportionate punishments among equally culpable offenders. A few of the clemency grants have been by governors who held serious concerns about capital punishment generally. Occasionally an outgoing governor will grant clemency to several death row inmates: New Mexico's Governor Anaya commuted six in 1986, Ohio's Governor Celeste commuted eight in 1991, and Illinois' Governor Ryan commuted all inmates in 2003, as did New Jersey Governor Corzine.

§ 14.2   Prisoner's Eligibility for Execution

Assume now that the condemned murderer has reached the very end of legal challenges to his death sentence: denied relief on appeal, in state collateral proceedings, in federal habeas corpus, and in the request for clemency. The governor has signed a death warrant ordering his execution no later than a date certain, and the prison officials are moving full speed ahead to conduct that execution. Only a few final glitches might delay or derail that final stage of the death penalty process.

Before a condemned prisoner can actually be executed, he must be "eligible" for execution. We know that the prisoner is eligible in the primary sense that he has been convicted of a capital crime, has been sentenced to death, and has exhausted all legal challenges to that conviction and death sentence. Roughly 10% or more of death row prisoners "volunteer" for execution, in that they refuse either to present a defense during the trial process or to pursue appeals and collateral attacks after the trial. If reasons exist making them "ineligible" for execution, such volunteers do not help to bring those reasons to the forefront. However, the vast majority of death row inmates do not go to their executions willingly, even though they may have tried to prepare themselves for their unavoidable deaths through final meetings with family and friends, last sessions of religious counseling, etc.

Perhaps the most common eleventh-hour claim is that the condemned murderer has become insane while on death row. He must not have been insane at the time of the crime, or presumably he would have been found not guilty by reason of insanity. He also must have been found mentally competent to face trial, or he wouldn't have been tried and convicted. If the sentencing stage raised mitigating circumstances of mental problems, they must have been insufficient to outweigh whatever aggravating circumstances were proven. Therefore, the essence of the argument at this final stage is that the death row prisoner has become insane since the trial process ended, as long as ten to over twenty years ago.

This issue is of considerable moment, since the Supreme Court has held that the 8th Amendment forbids the execution of the presently insane. *Ford v. Wainwright*, 477 U.S. 399, 106 S.Ct. 2595, 91 L.Ed.2d 335 (1986). Anglo–American common law has always prohibited execution of the insane, and all death penalty statutes prohibit it as well. *Ford* did not change this centuries-old legal principle but simply raised it to the constitutional level. The many reasons given for this conclusion include "to protect the condemned from fear and pain without comfort of understanding" and "to protect the dignity of society itself from the barbarity of exacting mindless vengeance."

The difficulty faced by the Supreme Court in *Ford* was not whether the insane could be executed but rather what minimal process must be provided for determining if the death row inmate is in fact currently insane. Florida had provided Alvin Ford only a psychiatric examination by the state's psychiatrists, disallowing any participation by Ford's lawyers or examination by defense psychiatrists. The psychiatric reports went directly to the governor who then had exclusive power to decide whether Ford was insane, all without including the death row prisoner or his attorneys in the determination process.

Ford held that basic due process rights apply to the determination of a death row prisoner's insanity prior to execution. Some members of the Supreme Court thought that meant a judicial hearing, and others thought that some sort of neutral fact-finding board would be sufficient. In any event, the prisoner must have the opportunity to be heard, to present his side of the case, and to be a full participant in the process for determining his sanity. *Ford* also did not provide a crystal-clear definition of what insanity is in this situation, other than to include such considerations as whether the prisoner is aware of where he is and why he was sentenced to death. In addition, Panetti v. Quarterman, ___ U.S. ___, 127 S.Ct. 2842, 168 L.Ed.2d 662 (2007) has asked whether the prisoner's gross delusions call into question that rational awareness.

If the death row prisoner is found to be sane, the governor can order his execution and the prison authorities can carry out that order. A bizarre alternative comes into play if the prisoner is found to be presently insane. The law forbids his execution until and unless he becomes sane sometime in the future for at least long enough to carry out the execution. This presumes that the prisoner will receive psychiatric treatment for his insanity, and, if he "gets well," his reward is to be executed by the state. Prisoner-patients undergoing such treatment might understandably be less than fully motivated to "get well." Such bizarre situations may be the ultimate example of the old saw that "the operation was a success, but the patient died!" These "operations" are unlikely to occur, given that such psychiatric treatment aiming to result in execution by the state is considered a violation of the codes of ethics for the treating therapist by the American Medical Association and the American Psychiatric Association.

Techniques for curing the death row prisoner for execution have other limits as well. *State v. Perry*, 610 So.2d 746 (La.1992), involved the case of a death row inmate who suffered from a mental illness that could not be cured on a permanent basis. However, if given a certain antipsychotic drug, he sometimes was able to function at a minimum level of rationality. The trial court had ordered that Perry be forcibly medicated (over his objections) until he could be executed. The Louisiana Supreme Court reversed that order and held that the state may not forcibly administer medication to a death row prisoner for the purposes of execution.

One obvious requirement for executing a death row prisoner is that the prisoner must still be alive. The many years of waiting on a death row while the death penalty system slogs through the case, means that a surprising number of such prisoners simply die on a death row either from natural causes or from being murdered by other inmates. Other death row prisoners attempt, sometimes successfully, to commit suicide before their date with the executioner. Given the premise of the state's need to conduct a dignified execution of the condemned prisoner, the prison authorities can be seen working hard to prevent suicide attempts and trying to save the life of any prisoner who does try to commit suicide, even just hours before the scheduled execution.

§ 14.3   Execution Methods and Procedures

In the current death penalty era (1973–present), only about 14% of all persons sentenced to death have actually been executed. Some of the others have "cheated the executioner" by dying of suicide, murder, or natural causes, but the most common result of being sentenced to death has been to have their death sentences reversed and be relegated to prison sentences. However, roughly 40% of all persons sentenced to death in the current era are still on death row, continuing to challenge their death sentence but realizing that some day their time may come.

The history of execution techniques down through the ages includes a wide array of bizarre and ghastly means of dispatching the condemned (see chapter 1). The first execution during the current era was that of Gary Gilmore in Utah on January 17, 1977, who died at the hands of a firing squad. Since that time, death row prisoners have been executed by hanging, electrocution, lethal gas, and lethal injection. However, by far the most common means of execution now is lethal injection, with the first such execution by lethal injection occurring in 1982 in Texas. As of 2005, Nebraska continued to authorize execution only by electrocution, but all other death penalty jurisdictions authorize lethal injection either as the sole means of execution or as one of two means that the prisoner may choose. In the early 21st century, the hypodermic needle and the hospital gurney are the icons of the death penalty, replacing past symbols including the electric chair, the hangman's noose, the firing squad, the guillotine, and the cross.

As the methods of executing prisoners have changed, attorneys for those prisoners have challenged, not surprisingly, the legality of any and all new methods. One of the most commonly cited cases is *In re Kemmler*, 136 U.S. 436, 105 S.Ct. 930, 34 L.Ed.2d 519 (1890). The New York legislature had just changed its means of execution from hanging to the electric chair, and the first execution by electric chair was about to take place. In *Kemmler*, the Supreme Court held that the 8th Amendment to the United States Constitution did not apply to the states and deferred to the judgment of the New York legislature that it was not cruel and unusual punishment. Despite *Kemmler*'s clear refusal to evaluate electrocution under the 8th Amendment, *Kemmler* nonetheless has often been cited mistakenly by other courts to dismiss challenges to the constitutionality of electrocution. However, the Nebraska Supreme Court recently held that electrocution violates the Nebraska Constitution. *State v. Mata*, 275 Neb. 1, 745 N.W.2d 229 (2008). As of 2008, electrocution is an authorized option for execution in only a few states.

Even before *Kemmler* had arisen, the Supreme Court had approved execution by firing squad. *Wilkerson v. Utah*, 99 U.S. (9 Otto) 130, 25 L.Ed. 345 (1878). Firing squads continue to be authorized only in Idaho and Utah. Hanging has not been evaluated by the Supreme Court during the current death penalty era, but the Ninth Circuit has upheld the constitutionality of hanging. *Campbell v. Wood*, 18 F.3d 662 (9th Cir.1994)(en banc), *cert. denied*, 511 U.S. 1119, 114 S.Ct. 2125, 128 L.Ed.2d 682 (1994). As of 2008, only New Hampshire and Washington permit hanging as an option for execution. Lethal gas (the gas chamber) has met with mixed constitutional reviews, being found acceptable in two circuits, *Hunt v. Nuth*, 57 F.3d 1327 (4th Cir. 1995), *cert. denied*, 516 U.S. 1054, 116 S.Ct. 724, 133 L.Ed.2d 676 (1996) and *Gray v. Lucas*, 710 F.2d 1048 (5th Cir.1983), *cert. denied*, 463 U.S. 1237, 104 S.Ct. 211, 77 L.Ed.2d 1453 (1983). However, the Ninth Circuit has found that lethal gas is cruel and unusual punishment under the 8th Amendment. *Fierro v. Gomez*, 77 F.3d 301 (9th Cir.1996). Lethal gas remains an option, along with lethal injection, only in a few states.

Essentially every death penalty jurisdiction has now moved to lethal injection as its exclusive or optional means of executing condemned prisoners, so the above-described challenges to other forms of execution are primarily of historical interest only. Lethal injection has displaced those other forms of execution largely because of the greatly reduced cost and minimal need for expensive facilities, and because lethal injection is seen as more humane and less likely to inflict unnecessary pain in getting to the end result.

The Supreme Court considered a related issue in *Heckler v. Chaney*, 470 U.S. 821, 105 S.Ct. 1649, 84 L.Ed.2d 714 (1985). In *Chaney*, death row inmates in Oklahoma and Texas had petitioned the United States Food and Drug Administration (FDA), claiming that the drugs being used for lethal injection had not been approved by the FDA as "safe and effective" for human executions, including the need for "warning labels." The Supreme Court in *Chaney* held that the FDA had discretion not to undertake enforcement action, and thus the FDA decision was not amenable to judicial review.

A major constitutional challenge to lethal injection was mounted in *Baze v. Rees*, ___ U.S. ___, 128 S.Ct. 1520, 170 L.Ed.2d 420 (2008). However, *Baze* became limited to questions about the acceptable risk of unnecessary pain and suffering during lethal injection. The Supreme Court in *Baze* did finally hold that lethal injection is not prohibited as Cruel and Unusual Punishment under the 8th Amendment, but these complex issues generated separate opinions from seven Justices leaving us far from a consensus. The specific three-drug protocol used in Kentucky was approved in *Baze*, but the applicability of this approval to other states using somewhat different protocols is unclear.

The prisoner's actual execution follows the governor's signing of a death warrant, essentially an executive order from the governor to the prison warden to execute a certain death row prisoner on or before a certain date. Prison officials then put into motion a carefully planned and well-rehearsed process to carry out this order. A step-by-step, often hour-by-hour schedule is initiated several days prior to the actual execution, and most death penalty states have detailed, written protocols for such activities. The execution takes place inside the maximum security prison, and the entire occasion is a solemn procedure. Often one sees animated, sometimes raucous demonstrations outside the prison by groups in favor of and groups opposed to the execution, but inside the prison all is quiet and decorous. The official witnesses to the execution are permitted to see the prisoner for only the few minutes needed for the actual termination of his life and not all of the days of elaborate preparations.

Executions are no longer public, but a few witnesses to the execution are selected from the victim's family, the offender's family, the press, and governmental officials. Executions take place deep in the bowels of maximum security prisons, making attendance by large crowds of people simply impossible. Much harder to justify is the blanket prohibition of photographing, filming, or televising executions. Print media representatives typically are present at the execution, and they can and do write textual descriptions of what occurred, but no court has yet held that members of the press or anyone else has a right to bring cameras or video equipment into the viewing room. Some courts have cited the prisoner's right to privacy, but this principle has been upheld even when the prisoner himself was the party seeking photographing, filming, and/or videotaping of his own execution. Prison officials have cited the disruption that camera equipment would cause, but a modern mini-cam positioned behind a one-way mirror seems unlikely to cause any disruption. Supporters of extended press access have argued that a government acting intentionally and premeditatedly to take the life of a human being is of extraordinary significance and should be subjected to broad public scrutiny. Others have noted that broad public viewing of executions might increase the general deterrent impact of such executions. However, lethal injections of prisoners are not nearly as dramatic or shocking as what one can view daily on television news shows or PG–13 movies, so actual executions seem unlikely to be memorable even if they were televised during prime time.

The typical procedure for lethal injections is for the prisoner to have an intravenous catheter inserted into an arm if possible, otherwise into whatever vein found to be usable. In a typical lethal injection process, the first step is to start a saline solution to flush the tubing and keep it unclogged. The first chemical injected is sodium thiopental (Sodium Pentothal), a frequently used anesthetic for surgery. This first drug is intended to induce a deep sleep and the loss of consciousness, usually in about 20 seconds. The second chemical is pancuronium bromide (Pavulon), a muscle relaxant which is intended to paralyze the diaphragm and lungs. The third drug injected is potassium chloride, often used also for heart bypass surgery but used here to induce cardiac arrest and to stop the subject's heart permanently. With the person's lungs paralyzed and heart permanently stopped, death follows rather quickly. A physician is present at all executions to pronounce the death of the prisoner who has been executed.

Serious problems arose when using former means of executing prisoners. The bodies of those electrocuted in electric chairs had to cool before they could be handled by the guards. The use of gas chambers to asphyxiate condemned prisoners required elaborate systems to evacuate the gas from the airtight chamber, replace it with clean air, and not expel the lethal gas anywhere that it could be harmful. Prisoners who die from lethal injection on hospital gurneys provide the fewest difficult and unpleasant tasks for those who must clean up after the ceremony is over.

Once the prisoner is dead, his or her remains are given to the family of the deceased for them to take care of as they wish, typically in a private funeral back home. If no friends or family members are available to receive the body, it will be buried in a prison cemetery or a potter's field somewhere nearby. Next morning's local newspapers and television news broadcasts report the execution, and, in rare cases, some national and international media coverage may also result. Lawyers, judges, and others who may have worked on this case for a decade or longer, now turn to their other clients and other cases. Family members of the executed offender and of the victim(s) are urged to put all of this behind them, to reach closure, and to get on with their lives. The issues in this case which burned so brightly and seemed so important now disappear. Nothing moots a case like an execution.

*

PART V
SPECIAL DEATH PENALTY ISSUES

CHAPTER 15

ASSISTANCE OF DEFENSE COUNSEL

A major problem with the operating death penalty system is the uneven quality of defense attorneys across the hundreds of states and counties in the United States. A few jurisdictions have high standards, reasonable compensation, and strong support systems for capital defense counsel. At the other extreme, many cases have inexperienced or incompetent attorneys assigned to capital cases with minimal fees and no support. Most disturbing are the many reported cases of defense attorneys being asleep or drunk during key parts of the trials and sentencing hearings. In almost all of these cases, our appellate review courts have affirmed the resulting convictions and death sentences despite this obviously unprofessional conduct. Although every capital defendant has the constitutional right to the effective assistance of counsel for his defense, we apparently have an appalling low standard for measuring effective assistance of counsel.

§ 15.1 Constitutional Right to Counsel

Successfully navigating the complex, often Byzantine death penalty system without the guiding hand of competent and experienced defense counsel would be nearly impossible even for the most astute capital defendant. If this defendant can afford six-figure legal fees, then he or she need never face that journey alone. However, almost no capital defendants can afford to pay such legal fees to hire private counsel, so they must fall back on public largess. Public funds can and will pay for defense attorneys who are appointed by trial courts to represent defendants in death penalty cases, but the defendant first must have a constitutional right to such appointed counsel.

The first case in which the Supreme Court recognized such a constitutional right was *Powell v. Alabama*, 287 U.S. 45, 53 S.Ct. 55, 77 L.Ed. 158 (1932). *Powell* involved seven young black men (''the Scottsboro boys'') convicted on questionable evidence of a gang rape of a white girl and sentenced to death at trials essentially without defense attorneys. The Supreme Court relied upon the due process clause of the 14th Amendment to find a requirement for the appointment of defense counsel to represent indigent capital defendants in such cases. However, the Court limited this right to counsel to death penalty cases with facts similar to those in *Powell*, where the capital defendants were described by the Court as "ignorant and illiterate" young black men, far away from home and facing a particularly hostile community environment. It was to be another 30 years before all capital defendants were guaranteed defense counsel in state criminal trials, but in practice state trial judges were fairly liberal in finding *Powell*-like situations and appointing defense counsel for capital defendants in most cases. In this mid–20th century era, that meant appointing private attorneys who were members of the local bar and who were willing to accept such appointments either pro bono or for the very low fees courts could offer. Nothing like the public defender offices of the early 21st century existed back then, so the local bar shouldered the burden.

The 6th Amendment provides that, "in all criminal prosecutions, the accused shall enjoy the right . . . to have the Assistance of Counsel for his defense." Given that the 6th Amendment applies directly to criminal prosecutions in federal courts, it is not surprising that soon after *Powell* the Supreme Court required federal courts to provide indigent defendants with appointed defense counsel in all felony cases, obviously including death penalty cases. *Johnson v. Zerbst*, 304 U.S. 458, 58 S.Ct. 1019, 82 L.Ed. 1461 (1938). However, only a few years later, the Supreme Court held that *Johnson* and the 6th Amendment did not apply to state criminal prosecutions. *Betts v. Brady*, 316 U.S. 455, 62 S.Ct. 1252, 86 L.Ed. 1595 (1942).

Then came the blockbuster case of *Gideon v. Wainwright*, 372 U.S. 335, 83 S.Ct. 792, 9 L.Ed.2d

799 (1963). *Gideon* directly overruled *Betts*, holding that 14th Amendment due process incorporated the 6th Amendment's right to counsel. Therefore, state courts must make appointed counsel available to indigent defendants in all felony cases, again obviously including death penalty cases. *Gideon* continues to be the foundation for providing appointed counsel during the trial process, and in a companion case the Supreme Court also required appointed counsel for the convicted defendant at the first appeal of right. *Douglas v. California*, 372 U.S. 353, 83 S.Ct. 814, 9 L.Ed.2d 811 (1963). In later appeals and collateral challenges, no constitutional right to appointed counsel exists. *Murray v. Giarratano*, 492 U.S. 1, 109 S.Ct. 2765, 106 L.Ed.2d 1 (1989); *Ross v. Moffitt*, 417 U.S. 600, 94 S.Ct. 2437, 41 L.Ed.2d 341 (1974); *Barbour v. Allen*, 471 F.3d 1222 (11th Cir. 2006), cert. denied, 127 S.Ct. 2996, 168 L.Ed.2d 707 (2007).

By far the majority of defense counsel appointed under *Gideon* and *Douglas* are criminal lawyers employed by public defender's offices and who receive regular paychecks from the same government entity that issues paychecks to the judge and to the prosecuting attorney. Public defenders may be augmented by private defense attorneys who are available for appointment to represent indigent defendants. In a typical jurisdiction, public defenders and their private counsel colleagues are quite experienced in routine criminal cases. However, death penalty cases are extremely unusual criminal cases, involving many issues not found in other criminal prosecutions, so often it is difficult to find appointed counsel who are experienced death penalty defense attorneys.

Given repeated statements by the Supreme Court that "death is different" and that very careful measures are needed in capital cases, one might have assumed that the qualifications and performance standards for death penalty lawyers would be higher than for defense lawyers representing clients accused of shoplifting or jaywalking. Not so, according to the Supreme Court in *Strickland v. Washington*, 466 U.S. 668, 104 S.Ct. 2052, 80 L.Ed.2d 674 (1984). David Washington was accused of committing a series of murders, tortures, kidnapings, and assaults, and the Florida trial court appointed an experienced criminal lawyer to represent him. Washington repeatedly acted against his counsel's advice, pleading guilty and waiving his rights to trial and to jury involvement in choosing between life in prison or a death sentence. Washington did want certain evidence presented to the sentencing judge, but his lawyer decided not to introduce that evidence at the sentencing hearing in order to keep out other damaging evidence. Washington was sentenced to death and appealed that sentence, claiming that his court-appointed defense counsel did not provide effective assistance of counsel.

In *Strickland*, the Supreme Court held that the standard to which appointed counsel are to be held is the same for death penalty cases as it is for other criminal cases, and that standard is "effective assistance of counsel." In order for a court on appeal or upon collateral review to find that the lawyer's trial-level performance was ineffective under the 6th Amendment, the defendant must prove first that the attorney's acts or omissions were "outside the range of professionally competent assistance" as compared to an "objective standard of reasonableness." Even if the defendant can prove that trial counsel's performance was unreasonable under this competence prong, the defendant must then prove the second prong, that "there is a reasonable probability that, but for counsel's unprofessional errors, the result of the proceeding would have been different." In making these assessments, "a court must indulge a strong presumption that counsel's conduct falls within the wide range of reasonable professional assistance."

Along with *Strickland*, the Supreme Court decided the companion case of *United States v. Cronic*, 466 U.S. 648, 104 S.Ct. 2039, 80 L.Ed.2d 657 (1984). Here it was observed that the original appointment of counsel could be so defective as to be treated as a per se violation of a criminal defendant's 6th Amendment right. However, assuming that the original appointment of counsel passes constitutional muster, then the assessment of effectiveness turns to counsel's actual performance at trial. The role of defense counsel is seen in *Cronic* as to assure "fairness in the adversary process" by confronting the prosecution's case and subjecting it to the "crucible of meaningful adversarial testing."

Despite, or perhaps because of, the standards for appointed counsel laid out in *Strickland* and *Cronic*, the Supreme Court and almost all lower courts have been very reluctant to find that the performance of appointed counsel in criminal cases was "ineffective" under the 6th Amendment. A large part of the reason for this has been the second prong of *Strickland*, requiring proof of a reasonable probability that the result would have been different if appointed counsel's performance had been up to par. In many death penalty cases, evidence of the defendant's guilt is very strong and several aggravating circumstances exist upon which a death sentence might rest. Combined with a court's "strong presumption" of reasonable performance by defense counsel, criminal defendants on appeal or on collateral review have seldom been able to prove both incompetence of their trial lawyer and prejudice resulting from that incompetence.

Both *Cronic* and *Strickland* have been affirmed repeatedly, including recently in *Bell v. Cone*, 535 U.S. 685, 122 S.Ct. 1843, 152 L.Ed.2d 914 (2002). *Cone* upheld the performance of appointed defense counsel in a death penalty case from Tennessee, even though counsel's "shortcomings included a failure to interview witnesses who could have provided mitigating evidence; a failure to introduce available mitigating evidence; and the failure to make any closing argument or plea for his client's life at the conclusion of the penalty phase." Chief Justice Rehnquist's majority opinion in *Cone* intoned *Strickland* to remind us "that a court must indulge a 'strong presumption' that counsel's conduct falls within the wide range of reasonable professional assistance because it is all too easy to conclude that a particular act or omission of counsel was unreasonable in the harsh light of hindsight." Under *Cone*, the inadequacy of defense counsel's performance has to be so extreme as to amount to not just bad lawyering but the equivalent of an absence of lawyering. Otherwise, the defendant must prove the second prong of the *Strickland* test, a reasonable probability that the case would have come out differently.

The Supreme Court's recent major venture into this area is in *Wiggins v. Smith*, 539 U.S. 510, 123 S.Ct. 2527, 156 L.Ed.2d 471 (2003). This was a death penalty case in which experienced defense attorneys decided to put almost all of their efforts into proving that the defendant was not directly responsible for the murder and to forego any significant effort to present mitigating evidence on his behalf. These defense attorneys, however, did not investigate the available mitigating evidence before making this decision not to use it. The Supreme Court noted that extensive and significant mitigating evidence was available in this case and, if it had been introduced, might well have convinced the jury not to recommend the death penalty. Therefore, the Court concluded that both *Strickland* prongs were violated: defense counsel's performance was inadequate and that inadequate performance may well have caused the jury to recommend death. *Wiggins* does not set a higher standard for capital defense counsel than for other defense counsel, but it does emphasize their special responsibilities in death penalty cases. The duty to investigate and evaluate mitigating evidence in death penalty cases is clearly imposed by *Wiggins*, and this dimension of capital defense is the most unique to capital cases.

Even before getting to the question of whether the defense attorney did a reasonable job, one might expect the attorney at least to have been awake during key parts of the trial. This frequently-condemned image of the sleeping defense attorney has come under attack in such cases as *Javor v. United States*, 724 F.2d 831 (9th Cir.1984), holding that "[w]hen a defendant's attorney is asleep during a substantial portion of the trial, the defendant has not received the legal assistance necessary to defend his interests at trial." Comparing the sleeping defense attorney to the reasonable performance standard, courts have observed that "the buried assumption in our *Strickland* cases is that counsel is present and conscious to exercise judgment, calculation and instinct, for better or worse. But that is an assumption we cannot make when counsel is unconscious at critical times." *Tippins v. Walker*, 77 F.3d 682 (2d Cir.1996). However, if the defendant objected to his defense attorney's attempts to present mitigating evidence at his original sentencing hearing, then he has a more difficult case to make during subsequent challenges to his resulting death sentence. *Schriro v. Landrigan*, ___ U.S. ___, 127 S.Ct. 1933, 167 L.Ed.2d 836 (2007). Even if another evidentiary hearing were scheduled, there is no reason to assume, the *Landrigan* Court held, that the now death-sentenced inmate won't object to presentation of mitigating evidence at that hearing at well.

A high profile case from Texas raised this same issue in *Burdine v. Johnson*, 262 F.3d 336 (5th Cir.2001), *cert. denied sub nom*, *Cockrell v. Burdine*, 535 U.S. 1120, 122 S.Ct. 2347, 153 L.Ed.2d 174 (2002). During Calvin Burdine's death penalty trial, his court-appointed defense attorney "repeatedly dozed or slept as the State questioned witnesses and presented evidence supporting its case against Burdine" during the guilt stage of the trial process. In *Burdine*, the federal district court had observed that "sleeping counsel is equivalent to no counsel at all," and the Fifth Circuit agreed, reversing Burdine's capital murder conviction. Despite being petitioned loudly and aggressively by the Texas attorney general to reverse the Fifth Circuit's decision, the Supreme Court denied certiorari without comment. *Cockrell v. Burdine*, 535 U.S. 1120, 122 S.Ct. 2347, 153 L.Ed.2d 174 (2002). While the Supreme Court's silence has no official significance as to the merits of a particular argument, this denial of certiorari was interpreted by the national media as the Supreme Court's unwillingness even to suggest that it is acceptable for a defense attorney to sleep through a trial, particularly in a death penalty case.

§ 15.2 Unique Role in Death Penalty Cases

The signal importance of defense attorneys in criminal cases begins with the language of the 6th Amendment: "in all criminal prosecutions, the accused shall enjoy the right ... to have the Assistance of Counsel for his defense." There is no comparable constitutional right for government entities to have a prosecuting attorney to assist or represent the state's interests in criminal prosecutions. However, every state does provide prosecuting attorneys, paid out of public funds, to represent the state in any and all criminal prosecutions, whether or not the defendant is represented by counsel.

The 6th Amendment right to counsel has not quite been extended to "all criminal prosecutions" but nearly so. *Gideon v. Wainwright*, 372 U.S. 335, 83 S.Ct. 792, 9 L.Ed.2d 799 (1963) provided this right to all felony cases, and the Supreme Court has recently extended this right to all criminal offenses, even minor misdemeanors, for which any incarceration at all is authorized. *Alabama v. Shelton*, 535 U.S. 654, 122 S.Ct. 1764, 152 L.Ed.2d 888 (2002). Within this spectrum of "all criminal prosecutions," death penalty cases are at the very top. Death cases involve the most horrible crimes, the "worst of the worst" offenders, and the most severe criminal sanction permitted by law. The oddity, then, is not that capital defendants have a constitutional right to counsel, but that the level of performance required under the 6th Amendment is identical for all defense attorneys, whether their clients face death or only one day in jail.

Some aspects of the role of defense attorneys in death cases are unique, but much of what they do is the same as for most other felony cases before a trial jury. All defense attorneys research the facts and law of their case, participate in jury selection, make opening and closing arguments to that jury, introduce and challenge physical evidence, examine and cross-examine witnesses, and attend to the many other demands of trying a case to a jury. The pressure of a jury trial, and the seemingly endless number of things to worry about, are indeed substantial in any felony case.

Death cases add to this normal role for the criminal trial lawyer several other important and unique responsibilities. From the very beginning of the defense attorney's involvement, the focus must be divided between preparation for the guilt stage and preparation for the sentencing stage. This is not true for essentially any other criminal case, because the defense attorney's role in sentencing is much less pronounced and can be initiated only some time after any conviction. In death cases, the defense attorneys (and the prosecuting attorneys as well) must prepare for an entire "second trial" on whether their client should live or die, to follow immediately after any conviction of the defendant of a capital crime. The mind set of many criminal trial attorneys is to be a "true believer" that they will win an acquittal in the guilt stage and to absolutely refuse to think about what might happen if they were to lose. Preparing for the sentencing stage even before the guilt stage has begun is psychologically difficult for them to do. If the jury returns a verdict of guilty to one or more capital crimes at the end of the guilt stage, the defense attorney typically is completely spent, exhausted from putting everything he or she had into the preceding guilt trial. The prospect of launching into a full-scale sentencing hearing, either immediately or tomorrow morning at the latest, is akin to a runner starting out to run a second marathon only minutes after completing the first marathon.

Beyond this preparation and scheduling nightmare, defense attorneys in death penalty cases must be able to gather evidence and prepare legal cases on the issue of life or death sentencing. Most felony trial defense attorneys are perfectly competent in guilt stage proceedings, attacking the constitutionality of the confession and of the seized evidence, but they have little if any experience in gathering and putting together evidence as to the appropriate sentence. It is common, therefore, for death penalty lawyers to work with mitigation specialists who do much of this work for them.

Another nearly unique dimension of a death case is the need to constantly keep an eye on the sentencing ramifications of everything that happens prior to the actual sentencing hearing itself. From the earliest stages of the case, often as soon as the crime is discovered and before the alleged offender is arrested, the media, the police, and the prosecuting attorney begin to talk about the death penalty. By the time the defense attorney is actually appointed, the judge will have entered a "gag order" for the lawyers so that they cannot discuss the case in the media, but the media drumbeat for the death penalty will continue. By the time jury selection begins, long before the defendant has been convicted of any capital crime(s), prospective jurors will be questioned carefully about their views on the death penalty (see chapter 9). Both the prosecuting attorney and the defense attorney are already into their dance for life or death, so what is said and done at the jury selection stage will come back either to haunt them or to reward them at the sentencing stage. Evidence presented and considered at the guilt stage also has implications for sentencing, and entire defense strategies at the guilt stage are devised to pay dividends at the sentencing stage. The prosecutor's pounding the jury on the most gruesome facts of the homicide has little to do with guilt and more to do with what punishment the offender should receive if found guilty. All of these factors mean that a key responsibility of the defense attorney in a death penalty case is to work with one eye on the issue of the moment and with the other eye on whether the defendant should live or die.

The trial attorney in a death case must also be constantly working to raise and preserve any and all constitutional challenges to evidence, events, and procedures prior to and during the entire trial process. This means that the death penalty trial attorney must have a thorough knowledge of all of the intricacies of the substantive and procedural law of the death penalty, as well as knowing when and how to raise them before and during the trial process. Otherwise, these issues typically are foreclosed from being raised on appeal or during collateral review.

Moving from the trial level to state appellate review and to state and federal collateral attacks, a lawyer representing the now convicted and death-sentenced defendant must have special knowledge above and beyond that of other criminal lawyers working at this post-trial level. Essentially all issues must be raised, completely and promptly, during the first stages, or they will be precluded from being raised in the later stages. Additional factual investigation often is necessary, particularly as to the defendant's character and background, and little time is allotted in which to do this. The most common issue raised in post-trial proceedings is the ineffectiveness of the trial counsel under *Strickland v. Washington*, 466 U.S. 668, 104 S.Ct. 2052, 80 L.Ed.2d 674 (1984). Basically, this requires one criminal lawyer trying to prove that another criminal lawyer performed incompetently. It is not unusual, for example, for an appellate public defender to be highly critical of the trial-level public defender who handled the case at trial and who works just down the hall from his critic.

Probably the most constant and persistent difference for defense attorneys in death cases is the very high profile, media-intense nature of such cases. To resort to a sports analogy, a felony case is akin to the big game on Saturday but a death penalty case is the superbowl and the world series all in one. The pressure is intense and the media attention is relentless. Constantly on the defense attorney's mind is that the client's very life is in your hands. Nothing else is comparable in the entire universe of the legal profession.

§ 15.3   Problems and Solutions

The most vocal critics of the death penalty system and of the death penalty itself have long decried the ubiquitous problem of defense attorneys in death cases who are grossly underpaid, shockingly inexperienced, denied funding for experts to assist them, and chosen too often from the bottom of the barrel of the local bar. Stories abound not only of sleeping lawyers but of corrupt and incompetent lawyers with serious drug and alcohol problems who struggle just to get out of bed in the morning, let alone put on a trial for life for a capital defendant.

Others, less suspect in their motivations, have begun to voice their concerns as well. In 2001, Ruth Ginsberg, Associate Justice of the United States Supreme Court, observed: "I have yet to see a death case, among the dozens coming to the Supreme Court on the eve of execution petitions, in which the defendant was well represented at trial." Also in 2001, Justice Sandra Day O'Connor volunteered in a speech: "Perhaps it's time to look at minimum standards for appointed counsel in death cases." Justice O'Connor went on to write the Court's opinion in *Wiggins* in 2003, but she did not take that final step of holding that the 6th Amendment requires higher minimum standards in death cases than in noncapital cases.

The most glaring problems may be a lack of information and education, a lack of staff and funding, and unnecessary pressure to hurry the death case through regardless of the defense attorney's ability to keep up. The first problem may be on its way to solution. A growing number of law schools are offering courses on the death penalty, with strong casebooks and supplemental materials. Continuing legal education (CLE) on death penalty issues is also growing in availability and sophistication, so that death penalty defense attorneys can learn and relearn the basics as well as the latest developments. One used to see a steady stream of cases in which the trial attorney didn't realize that a separate sentencing hearing was to follow the guilt stage or that didn't raise basic points about the defendant's character and background at that sentencing hearing, but such gross errors now seem to be less common. This may be in part because of the widespread availability of law school and CLE death penalty courses, but it is also in part because some death penalty states are requiring such courses before a member of the bar is eligible to be appointed as defense counsel in a death case.

The lack of staff and funding for the defense in death penalty cases may be much harder to resolve. These cases are already extraordinarily expensive and rarely result in actual execution, so the price tag per execution in most death penalty states is at least several million dollars, many times what life imprisonment would cost. Diverting even more tax dollars to the defense of our "worst of the worst" murderers may be neither likely nor desirable. The problem comes in part from the level of staffing and funding for the state in death cases, including the entire investigative arm of the police department, the experienced criminal trial lawyers working for the prosecuting attorney's office, the crime labs and forensic experts available to support the efforts of the prosecuting attorney, etc. Matching all of that for the defense is simply not in the cards. However, a trend can be seen among death penalty states to provide more realistic fee scales for defense attorneys, to provide funds for investigators, mitigation specialists, expert witnesses, and others to help put together the case for the defense. Given the holding in *Wiggins* (2003), a serious investigation and analysis of mitigating evidence must be conducted by the defense, so this is no longer really optional. Of course, all of this continues to drive up the overall cost of capital punishment to the community, fueling the question of whether such an expensive and, many would say, ineffective governmental program is worth it.

Finally, both courts and legislatures continue to create pressure to hurry death cases through regardless of the defense attorneys' ability to keep up. Part of the motivation for this development is that death cases take so many years, sometimes decades, to get from the death sentence being imposed at trial and to the condemned prisoner finally being executed. Another source of this pressure comes from the conclusion (or at least the fear) that death penalty lawyers do everything they can to delay the case, to bog it down whenever possible, and generally to keep their client alive long beyond when the state thinks he should have been dispatched by their executioner. The deadly punctuation to this pressure to hurry is that missed deadlines result in a loss of consideration of the issues that would have been raised by the defendant.

Solutions or at least reactions to these problems might come from three primary sources. First, if Justice O'Connor's unofficial musings are taken as a harbinger of things to come, the Supreme Court may need to revisit one of the holdings of *Strickland v. Washington*, 466 U.S. 668, 104 S.Ct. 2052, 80 L.Ed.2d 674 (1984) that the minimum constitutional standard for the performance of defense attorneys appointed to represent defendants in death penalty cases is no different from that for any other criminal case. Now that exact same right to counsel is extended to any criminal defendant facing even one day in jail (*Alabama v. Shelton*, 535 U.S. 654, 122 S.Ct. 1764, 152 L.Ed.2d 888 (2002)), holding them both to the same standard seems difficult to justify. *Wiggins* (2003) is a step in that direction, but more may be needed.

The second source of solutions to these problems is the courts of last resort in death penalty jurisdictions. A significant trend appears to be developing for these state supreme courts to enact court rules requiring an enhanced level of qualification for court appointed defense counsel in death cases. Some jurisdictions, such as Ohio, even require that eligibility for such appointment must be certified by a state-level commission, empowered to investigate the credentials and background of members of the bar seeking eligibility. The third source of such actions can be the legislatures of death penalty jurisdictions, primarily as to enhanced funding made available to local jurisdictions for such expenses but also as to the variety of people and services than should be available.

CHAPTER 16

RACE, GENDER, AND OTHER BIASES

Our death penalty system is authorized to impose the most severe sanction permitted by American law only on the "worst of the worst" offenders who have committed the most horrible crimes. The Supreme Court has labored mightily to steer this lethal system away from considerations of race, sex, socioeconomic class, and other personal characteristics of the victims and offenders. However, the system functions daily within American society and is operated by police officers, investigators, lawyers, judges, and jurors who live in our communities. To the degree these biases permeate all of us in nearly everything we say and do, the death penalty system cannot be expected to escape their impact. This is the governmental process, however, that decides literally who lives and who dies, so we may be justified in holding it to higher standards than, say, a community process deciding who gets into law school, or who gets a job at the local factory, or who moves into the house next to us. In fact, the death penalty system is held to a much lower standard than any of those selection processes.

§ 16.1   Race Bias

Race bias has plagued the overall criminal justice system throughout the ages, often with criminal law being used not to achieve criminal justice but to oppress, isolate, and punish target racial groups. It is not surprising that this plague also has infected the death penalty system, a wholly-owned subsidiary of the criminal justice system. The result has been that a white life is valued more than a black life. The murder of a white victim is considered more egregious than the murder of a black victim, and the execution of a white offender is considered less appropriate than the execution of a black offender.

Early research on the impact of race in the criminal justice system in general and the death penalty system in particular focused almost solely upon the variable of race of offender, specifically comparing the conviction and death-sentencing rate for white and black offenders involved in similar crimes. The now-familiar findings were that black offenders were more likely to be sentenced to death than were white offenders, even for essentially the same crimes. Subsequent, more sophisticated research included analyses of the variable of race of victim, and even more striking differences were found. The murder of white victims is treated much more aggressively and harshly by the death penalty system than the murder of victims of color, regardless of the race or color of the offender. Leading studies have found that those who kill white victims are over four times as likely to be sentenced to death as those who kill black victims under otherwise the

same circumstances. The strongest race bias, therefore, comes into play when a black or Latino offender is accused of murdering a white victim. As
explained more fully in § 16.2 and § 16.3, the ultimate fast track to death row is reserved for a
young black homosexual male from the lowest social class who murders an older white heterosexual
grandmother from the highest social class.

Race bias has been a topic of concern for the
Supreme Court as well as for lower courts and
legislatures, ranging over many years and into a
wide variety of legal arenas. It has been a cloud
over death penalty cases as well, but only in the
current era (1973–present) has race bias been
pulled kicking and screaming out of those shadows
into the light of analysis. In *Furman v. Georgia*, 408
U.S. 238, 92 S.Ct. 2726 (1972), several members of
the Supreme Court began to voice their concerns.
Justice Douglas worried that the discretion of
judges and juries in imposing the death penalty
enables it to be selectively applied against a defendant who "is a member of a suspect and unpopular
minority." Justice Marshall in *Furman* pointed to
gross execution data and concluded: "Studies indicate that while the higher rate of execution among
Negroes is partially due to a higher rate of crime,
there is evidence of racial discrimination." Justice
Powell voiced cautious optimism: "The possibility of
racial bias in the trial and sentencing process has
diminished in recent years."

Well into the current death penalty era, the Supreme Court decided the case of a black defendant

convicted and sentenced to death for the murder of a white storekeeper. *Turner v. Murray*, 476 U.S. 28, 106 S.Ct. 1683, 90 L.Ed.2d 27 (1986). The Virginia trial judge had refused defense counsel's request to question prospective jurors during voir dire about racial prejudice. In *Turner*, the Supreme Court recognized that "[b]ecause of the range of discretion entrusted to a jury in a capital sentencing hearing, there is a unique opportunity for racial prejudice to operate but remain undetected." Finding an unacceptable risk that race bias played a role in the sentencing and noting the "complete finality of the death sentence," *Turner* held that a capital defendant accused of an interracial crime is entitled to have prospective jurors questioned as to race bias.

One year after *Turner*, the Supreme Court decided the landmark case of *McCleskey v. Kemp*, 481 U.S. 279, 107 S.Ct. 1756, 95 L.Ed.2d 262 (1987). The majority opinion in *McCleskey* was written by Justice Lewis Powell, who had dissented in *Turner*. Justice Powell's majority opinion in *McCleskey* reviewed a detailed empirical study of race bias affecting Georgia's death sentencing process, introduced into evidence in this case in which a black defendant was sentenced to death for killing a white police officer. *McCleskey* strove mightily to discredit this study but in the end did acknowledge that it "indicates a discrepancy that appears to correlate with race." The Supreme Court went on, however, to hold that, even assuming a pattern of race bias generally in Georgia, a capital defendant would have to prove in addition that race bias played a role in his specific conviction and/or death sentence. Such proof, presumably, would come only from a judge or juror admitting under oath that he or she discriminated based on racial factors in choosing to sentence the defendant to death. Given that such candid confessions of racism are extremely unlikely to be forthcoming, almost no capital defendant would be able to satisfy this burden.

The result for Warren McCleskey was that his conviction and death sentence were upheld by the Supreme Court. In a rare moment of candor for such an eminent jurist, Justice Powell said after his retirement that he had changed his mind and now thought his opinion in *McCleskey* was wrong. Indeed, Justice Powell went on to say that "I have come to think that capital punishment should be abolished [in all cases]." Justice Powell's retirement musings were made in 1991, the same year that the State of Georgia executed Warren McCleskey.

Following the holding in *McCleskey*, concern about race bias in the death penalty process turned to the promotion of new legislative initiatives which were to become known as Racial Justice Acts. These amendments to death penalty statutes would allow capital defendants to challenge their death sentences on appeal or in collateral review by marshaling statistical evidence of race bias. If the defendant can establish a presumption of race bias, it then falls to the state to prove that such general race bias has not infected this specific case. This latter provision is essentially the same burden of proof as that required by the Supreme Court in *McCleskey*, but it is given to the prosecution instead of to the defense. Kentucky enacted a Racial Justice Act in 1998, and the legislatures of many other states, as well as the United States Congress, have debated bills to enact such statutes. However, as of the early 21st century, Kentucky remains the only death penalty jurisdiction that has chosen this legislative alternative for combating race bias in the death penalty system. Moreover, the momentum behind this legislative effort seems to have waned, so the race bias issue within death penalty jurisprudence remains back at the *McCleskey* decision.

§ 16.2   Gender Bias

In addition to race bias, there exists a system-wide apparent bias based upon the sex of the offender and perhaps upon the sex of the victim. This apparent sex bias has been recognized at the highest levels, including by Justice Thurgood Marshall in his *Furman* opinion: "There is also overwhelming evidence that the death penalty is employed against men and not women.... It is difficult to understand why women have received such favored treatment since the purposes allegedly served by capital punishment seemingly are applicable to both sexes."

Justice Marshall's intuitive concern is bolstered by empirical data during the current death penalty era. Women are unlikely to be arrested for murder, only very rarely sentenced to death, and almost never executed. Men who are arrested for homicide are nearly seven times as likely to be sentenced to death as are women who commit homicide. This aggressive diversion of women who commit murder away from actual execution is nothing new. Of the more than 8,424 persons lawfully executed in United States from 1900 through 2007, only 50 (0.6%) were women.

These data provide the unmistakable appearance of sex bias in the death penalty system. Men are eight times as likely as women to be arrested for murder, seven-two times as likely to be sentenced to death, and 140 times as likely to be executed. Assumptions generated by such raw data are abetted by the informal comments of judges, jurors, and prosecutors over many decades, revealing their reluctance to execute women, at least as compared to executing men of the same culpability.

Imagine if data of similar proportions distinguished between murderers of different races instead of different sexes. What if a black man arrested for murder were 140 times as likely as a white man arrested for murder to actually be executed for his crime? One might suggest either that white men seem to be benefitting from this arrest-to-execution pattern or that black men are being executed far too frequently. The same analysis would apply in this sex bias analysis.

Do these data necessarily indicate sex bias in the death penalty system? A major part of the explanation for this disparity is that the under-representation of women on death row is actually a discounting of the seriousness of the sort of homicides women typically commit. That is, women's murders are more likely than those of men to be of intimates in domestic violence cases. The criminal justice system tends to treat domestic violence cases less harshly, resulting in fewer death penalties for the offender, no matter whether male or female. Since women are more commonly the victims of domestic violence than the perpetrators, the discounting of the seriousness of such cases actually works against women as a group more than it works to their advantage. This analysis undoubtedly has merit but explains only part of the differential.

Other factors beyond the domestic dimension may also have an impact. For example, typical aggravating circumstances in death penalty statutes include such considerations as the offender's prior record of violent crimes, potential for future violent acts, and premeditation of the capital murder. Women convicted of capital murder, compared to their male counterparts, are less likely to have these aggravating circumstances so strongly in their cases. The same effect results from several mitigating circumstances, such as whether the offender is perceived as having been under extreme emotional disturbance or the substantial domination of another when she killed. While women capital defendants fare better than men on these mitigating circumstances, it is suspected that such differences stem mostly from common public perceptions of women versus men rather than the realities of the individual case. In any event, aggravating and mitigating circumstances still account for only some and not all of the differential for men and women capital defendants.

If a plausible sex bias argument can be made, why not pursue this argument in the courts? Men on death row might argue, in essence, that they would not have been sentenced to death if they were women. Although it appears that an overall pattern of sex bias very likely could be proven, such litigation would run into the brick wall of *McCleskey v. Kemp*, 481 U.S. 279, 107 S.Ct. 1756, 95 L.Ed.2d 262 (1987). *McCleskey* requires not only proof of a pattern of discrimination but also that the death-sentenced inmate's specific case involved race discrimination. Evidence to prove this additional factor almost always must come from admissions of racial prejudice from sentencing judges and jurors, and such admissions would be extremely hard to elicit.

Assuming that the *McCleskey* test would be required in sex bias cases as in race bias cases, proving a pattern of discrimination would satisfy only the first step. The petitioner would have to prove in his case that sex bias was involved. Perhaps it would be more socially acceptable for a judge or juror to admit to special treatment of women over men, but it does seem nearly as difficult as obtaining admissions of race bias.

Much less probing research has been conducted on the importance of sex of victim in the death penalty system. However, extrapolating from the tendency to value women's lives more highly when it comes to executing offenders, one might venture that this higher value placed on the lives of women might result in a greater likelihood of receiving the death penalty if the victim is a woman. This assumption may be countered somewhat by the history of Anglo–American law allowing husbands to beat their wives and treating the wife comparable to a farm animal. Even without the careful empirical research that would be needed to answer this question, anecdotal information indicates that judges and juries are outraged most by the murder of a female victim, particularly a young girl or elderly woman. Indeed, age of victim seems to be a factor regardless of sex, in that the murder of a child or an elderly person is a greater shock to most communities than other homicides.

§ 16.3   Other Biases

Moving beyond the specific issues of race and sex, it seems clear that some human lives are simply valued less than others, at least when a sentencing judge or jury is deciding whether or not to terminate that life. Often closely associated with race, the factor of socioeconomic status appears to play a part. When a poor capital defendant confronts huge government agencies pushing for death, his or her inability to pay for the very best lawyers, experts, and investigators often resembles the neighborhood sandlot baseball team taking on the New York Yankees. Therefore, the apparent over-representation of the poor on death row may be nothing more than their inability to pay the fees and expenses of those who could have kept them off death row.

Obviously connected to economic class are educational level, career success, and, often, contributions to the community. These latter characteristics can be used effectively as mitigating circumstances in the sentencing stage of a death penalty trial, and they tend to be correlated more with those in the middle-class and upper-class than with others.

Another major factor about which we know far too little is sexual orientation of the offender and/or the victim. Again without systematic empirical research and having to rely primarily on anecdotal information, it appears that capital defendants who are gay or lesbian see their sexual orientation used subtly as an unspoken aggravating circumstance. Many jurors, certainly those from certain religious backgrounds, will strongly disapprove of such individuals and, therefore, may be even more willing to order that they be executed. In such cases, prosecutors seem to find ways to get in evidence of the defendant's homosexuality, even when it appears to have no connection to the crime at all. Similarly, if the victim is identified as anything other than heterosexual, his or her death may be seen as less of a loss to the community.

Finally, it is almost universally true that the lives of people who are different from us and people who are outsiders are less valuable to our community (and therefore to a jury selected from our community). A terrible tragedy resulting in hundreds of deaths in another country, or even in another city in the United States, seems to catch our attention less than the untimely death of "one of our own." If we value the lives of our "own people" more highly than the lives of "other people," then the drifter from far away who comes into our town and kills once of us will be condemned much more readily than otherwise might occur. If the defendant is of a different religion, ethnic background, or even life-style, the jury may tend to treat him or her as a "stranger." This tendency to dehumanize those who are different than us can be seen in our attitudes toward wartime enemies, toward foreign terrorists, and even toward "different" people who want to move into our neighborhood.

CHAPTER 17

EXECUTING THE INNOCENT

"The execution of a person who can show that he is innocent comes perilously close to murder," according to Justice Blackmun in *Herrera v. Collins*, 506 U.S. 390, 113 S.Ct. 853, 122 L.Ed.2d 203 (1993). We have executed the innocent nonetheless, either because he could not "show that he is innocent" or because we would not believe him. In a speech in July 2001, Justice O'Connor expressed our worst fears: "If the statistics are any indication, the system may well be allowing some innocent defendants to be executed." We have always feared that the system might make mistakes, that innocent people might be convicted of capital crimes, sentenced to death, and actually executed. Justice Souter expressed this concern in *Kansas v. Marsh*, 548 U.S. 163, 126 S.Ct. 2516, 165 L.Ed.2d 429 (2006): "the period starting in 1989 has seen repeated exonerations of convicts under death sentences, in numbers never imagined before the development of DNA tests." Any government system operated by imperfect human beings and handling thousands of cases each year is bound to make mistakes. If the mistake was to convict and imprison an innocent person, we can correct that mistake to some degree by freeing that prisoner and perhaps even compensating him for his years in prison. If we execute an innocent person, however, no form of compensation or correction seems adequate to correct our error.

§ 17.1   Categories of Innocence

Innocence mistakes occur at two primary levels. First, we have found cases in which the condemned prisoner simply had nothing to do with the crime. These are cases of completely mistaken identity, stemming commonly from inaccurate but convincing eyewitness testimony. Eyewitness misidentification is the most frequently cited cause of miscarriages of justice generally, and death penalty cases are no exception.

Instances in which completely innocent persons are convicted of capital crimes, sentenced to death, and actually executed are the most egregious errors of our death penalty system. Even within this most extreme category, however, we may find gradations. At one end of the spectrum would be those who had absolutely nothing to do with this murder, have never been involved in any way with any violent crime, and typically have no criminal record at all. They simply had enormous bad luck in being caught up in this death penalty investigation, trial, and execution. Obviously, imposing the death penalty upon members of this group is the most shocking and unforgivable.

At the other end of the spectrum might be the serial killer who freely confesses to a long string of murders but who did not commit the specific murder for which he is sentenced to death. Often he has even confessed to this specific murder, but he is either mistaken or suicidal. Some might say that a serial killer deserves the death penalty more than almost any other offender, and perhaps we should not be too concerned about connecting the execution to precisely the right murder. Most, however, would note that the criminal sanction imposed, whether death or some other sanction, must be as a direct result of conviction of a criminal offense, whether capital or some lesser crime. If the defendant is actually innocent of the crime for which he was convicted and sentenced to death, then no criminal sanction would be legally valid.

The second primary level of innocence mistakes involves individuals who were involved in the homicide, perhaps even the primary actor, but who nonetheless should not have been sentenced to death. This concept goes back to the fact that we execute only about 1% of all persons who commit homicide, presumably the "worst of the worst" such killers. Therefore, even though the defendant did actually kill the victim, he or she should have been relegated to the "bottom 99%" of all such killers and not actually executed for the homicide.

Such offenders often are labeled "innocent of the death penalty." This awkward phrase is meant to label those who may be guilty of murder but not of capital murder. For example, many death penalty jurisdictions distinguish between murder and capital murder by requiring the latter to involve such factors as multiple victims or the killing of a police officer acting in the line of duty. In cases in which several actors kill several victims, the defendant may be personally responsible for only one of the homicides. If that defendant is wrongly convicted of two or more of the homicides, resulting in a capital crime conviction, then any resulting death penalty would be inappropriate. This defendant is certainly not innocent of the murder which he did commit, but he is innocent of the capital crime of multiple murders. Therefore, he should have received a sentence, presumably a long prison term, solely for that single murder, and not a death sentence for the capital crime.

Another, much more common example of death row prisoners who are "innocent of the death penalty" are those properly convicted of capital crimes but who do not "deserve" the death penalty. This can result in death penalty jurisdictions that require weighing the aggravating circumstances against the mitigating circumstances during the sentencing stage of the trial process. In some cases, the aggravating circumstances relied upon by the sentencing jury were inaccurate or overstated, thus receiving a level of importance in the weighing process that they should not have been given. For example, in nearly all homicide cases, a skilled prosecuting attorney can paint a dramatic picture of the victim's presumed pain and horror as he or she faced death, of the unfathomable grief suffered by the victim's family and friends, and of our society's need to "send a message" that such violent deaths simply will not be tolerated. Even if informed of the 1% "worst of the worst" statistics, an individual sentencing jury would have no basis for comparison of this murder to other murders or knowing whether this particular murder is in the worst 1% or the other 99%. Any murder is infinitely horrible, so the jury may give great weight simply to the fact that this is a murder, in violation of the sentencing requirements of weighing aggravating and mitigating circumstances against each other.

In some death penalty cases, the defense simply falls down on the job. Some of the mitigating circumstances are either understated or entirely omitted, again preventing an accurate weighing process for the sentencing jury to undertake. In what appears to be the vast majority of death penalty cases, significant mitigating factors are either discovered or at least fully developed only after the trial process is completed. The sentencing jury never received this evidence and obviously did not include it in the weighing process. Attempts to raise this newly found evidence on appeal or during collateral review must be channeled into claims of ineffective assistance of counsel (see chapter 15), and they are almost never sufficient to gain a reversal of the death sentence. Therefore, the argument goes, the death sentence did not result from a full consideration and weighing of all relevant aggravating and mitigating circumstances. If such a process had occurred, the defendant might well not have been sentenced to death.

Another category of persons arguably "innocent of death" are those whose death sentences were based in part on their race, ethnicity, sex, sexual orientation, or other such factors. The assumption here is that the defendant did commit the capital murder and that a reasonable array of aggravating and mitigating circumstances were weighed in the balance, but one or more of these improper factors acted as a "thumb on the scale." In essence, if the defendant had not been black, or Muslim, or gay, he would not have been sentenced to death. Therefore, either he should not be on death row, or a huge number of white, Christian, heterosexuals who committed very similar murders should be there along with him. This "innocence" argument obviously relies more on fairness and equal protection assumptions than it does on an absence of legal guilt.

A final example, while a stretch, may be the death case defendant who has a sleeping defense attorney, a politically-ambitious prosecutor, a hanging judge, and a vengeful jury. Despite the call for fairness and equal treatment of death cases, each defendant usually is tried separately before a jury assembled just this one time for this one case and with a unique combination of defense attorney, prosecutor, and judge. The luck of the draw therefore plays a significant role in who does and does not get sentenced to death. The Supreme Court has recognized that "[a]ny capital sentencing scheme may occasionally produce aberrational outcomes," but it has imposed no constitutional requirement that a state appellate court compare the appropriateness of the death sentence in the case before it with the penalties imposed in similar cases. *Pulley v. Harris*, 465 U.S. 37, 104 S.Ct. 871, 79 L.Ed.2d 29 (1984). Death row inmates who have been the recipient of one of these "aberrational outcomes," while not exactly innocent, might well have not been sentenced to death under any other circumstances.

§ 17.2   Impact on Death Penalty System

No matter how much we try to perfect the death penalty system, we cannot make it error-free. If and when it unfairly imposes death sentences on certain kinds of defendants and not others, or even when it executes a minor player in the murder and not the actual triggerman, we may try to grin and bear it. However, when it imposes death sentences on those who are innocent, even the strongest supporters of the death penalty are appalled. Even though a jury has found the defendant guilty beyond a reasonable doubt, and court after court has reviewed the case, residual doubt as to the condemned prisoner's guilt continues to pester us. That fear of executing the innocent never quite goes away.

For the jurors during the trial process, they struggle with the evidence of guilt during the first stage, testing that evidence against a proof standard of beyond a reasonable doubt. If they convict the defendant and move on to the sentencing stage of the trial process, the defense may still ask them to keep in mind any residual or lingering doubt they may have as to the defendant's guilt (see § 11.2). Stressing that executing the defendant is an irreversible step, the defense attorney can be expected to play on the jurors' inherent uncertainty as to whether they are absolutely sure that they are right and that there is no chance they could be wrong. *Oregon v. Guzek*, 546 U.S. 517, 126 S.Ct. 1226, 163 L.Ed.2d 1112 (2006). Therefore, this lingering doubt, this residual fear of sending an innocent person to death row, can have an impact on a jury at sentencing.

Police and prosecuting attorneys must also struggle with the fear of "getting the wrong man." Remember that the murders that generate death penalty cases typically are particularly horrible and shocking crimes. Police and prosecutors receive enormous pressure from their superiors in political office, from the media, and often from the victim's family to catch the bad guy(s) and to seek the death penalty. Working in such an environment can and sometimes does result in making errors from moving too fast. Also, once the alleged murderer is arrested and charged, it would be professionally embarrassing to announce that a mistake had been made and that they had the wrong guy. This pressure to engage in a "rush to judgment" can result in overlooked evidence, unpursued witnesses, and downplayed alternate possibilities. Human behavior being what it is, police and prosecutors can be expected to repress these facts and to confidently announce to their supervisors, to the media, to the general public, and subsequently to the judge and jury, that they are certain they have the right person. Nevertheless, harboring at least a lingering doubt that the alleged murderer is innocent must give them pause in some cases.

The magic solution to the innocence problem being heralded since the mid–1990s is the use of DNA evidence to prove "once and for all" whether the defendant is innocent or not. Of course, the use of DNA evidence is not limited to death penalty cases, and it is very accurate in identifying the substance in question. Innocence projects have sprung up in law schools everywhere, engaging law students in the search for legal truth through physical science. However, only a small percentage of death penalty cases have appreciable amounts of DNA evidence to be tested, so this magic solution is simply irrelevant to the majority of cases. Another, much more annoying problem is that DNA evidence may not be carefully collected and analyzed by those with access to the crime scene. We also see instances of this evidence being destroyed by police and prosecutors after the trial is over, making subsequent defense challenges almost impossible to support.

Defense attorneys are required to represent their client's interests zealously, even when they are certain that their client committed the murder as alleged and deserves to die. Even the most experienced criminal defense attorneys can count on one hand the clients they have had who are completely innocent. Criminal defendants and convicted prisoners alike tend to claim that they are innocent even when the evidence against them is overwhelming. Defense attorneys learn to take such claims with at least a grain of salt and to expect their criminal clients to not be fully truthful with them. In criminal law, the defendant's plea of "not guilty" is more an assertion of the procedural right to have the government prove the case beyond a reasonable doubt than it is any substantive assertion of actual innocence. However, when a truly innocent criminal client does come along, the defense attorney can be expected to have renewed vigor in representing such a client. A more common halfway ground exists when the attorney believes the client committed the crime but that the mitigating circumstances are so strong that he should not be sentenced to death ("innocent of the death penalty").

For the death penalty system to function, the community at large must support it and have faith that it is fair and accurate. When and if that community begins to believe that innocent persons are being condemned to death, the death penalty system will come under intense scrutiny and may be unable to function at all. It is at that point that governors become receptive to appeals for clemency and legislators begin to consider restrictive statutory amendments. Moreover, public opinion polls and similar research instruments indicate that the fear of executing the innocent is a constant underlying theme of much greater significance than concerns about race bias or other problems with the system.

In rare instances, concerns over error and executing the innocent have completely stalled death penalty systems. One example was the March 2000 decision by Governor George Ryan of Illinois to declare a moratorium on executions. The Illinois governor's major concern was execution of the innocent: "Until I can be sure with moral certainty that no innocent man or woman is facing a lethal injection, no one will meet that fate." A blue ribbon commission was appointed to investigate the Illinois death penalty system and to recommend changes to avoid executing the innocent. The commission's report was released in 2002 and was considered as the basis for new death penalty legislation in the Illinois legislature. Other death penalty states also are either considering or have put in place a moratorium on executions until some major problems can be fixed, including the innocence issue.

Of course, requiring perfection would mean an end to the death penalty altogether. An unavoidable cost of doing business within the death penalty system is the execution of the innocent at least occasionally. Strong proponents of the death penalty have compared the unavoidable execution of the innocent to the tragic loss of innocent life on our nation's highways. While we strive to make driving as safe as possible, we understand and accept the fact that some innocent people will die. Nonetheless, this inherent drawback doesn't cause us to shut down our highway system and forbid people from driving. Similarly, we don't prohibit attacks on enemy strongholds during wartime just because a few innocent bystanders may die as a result of our attack. Neither, goes the argument, should we shut down our death penalty system just because some innocent people will die in our execution chambers.

If the overall program (be it highway travel, war, or the death penalty) is worthwhile enough, we must be willing to accept such costs of doing business.

§ 17.3 Avoiding Innocence Errors

Even if one sees the execution of innocent persons as an unavoidable and acceptable cost of doing business, presumably all would agree that we should do what we can to minimize those costs. The most obvious and effective changes are suggested in the descriptions earlier in this chapter of the many sources of this problem. The first category of solutions might be to assure that our very best police officers, prosecutors, defense attorneys, and judges are assigned to death penalty cases. Certainly as compared to any other criminal cases, death penalty cases are the superbowl and the world series wrapped up into one, and we need our very best professionals to carry them out. This means enhanced qualifications needed for such persons to work on death cases as compared to other felony cases, and it means higher salaries and expense accounts as well.

The second category of solutions might be to slow down the rush to judgment in death penalty cases. From the moment the crime is discovered, every actor in the process works in a pressure cooker to gather and analyze evidence, to build a case, and to move the case along. Even in the last stages of appeal and collateral review, the emphasis seems to be more on getting it over with than on getting it right. All of this time, the capital defendant is locked up in jail and not going anywhere, so the need for haste at the cost of accuracy seems difficult to appreciate. To be sure, many death penalty defense lawyers have made delay-for-the-sake-of-delay into a fine art, even on behalf of death row prisoners for whom innocence is not even an arguable issue. This means that trying to regulate the speed of the system may not be easy, but it may be preferable to the current approach.

A third approach is to identify the most common factors that result in errors of this nature and then change the system to counteract those factors. For example, we know that the primary factors in discovering that a person on death row is actually innocent are attention to the case by defense attorneys and others, subsequent confession by the actual perpetrator of the crime, post-trial recanting of testimony by key witnesses, documentation of an ironclad alibi for the death row prisoner, and just plain luck. We also know that DNA catches errors in only a handful of death row exonerations, but DNA evidence that is analyzed carefully by both the prosecution and defense would be a major step in the right direction.

The primary source of mistaken convictions, in death cases as well as other criminal trials, is eyewitness testimony. Even though careful research over several decades has proven the extreme unreliability of eyewitness identification, death penalty cases continue to rely upon it whenever it is available and juries treat it as gospel. Proposals have been made to ban eyewitness testimony from death cases, but none have been accepted. If we are to make a meaningful reduction of the number of innocent persons being sent to death row, this problem must be addressed. A related problem is the reliance upon confessions, particularly if the death case involves a young, immature, borderline mentally retarded, or mentally ill defendant. As unlikely as it seems to the rest of us, for some a confession to an infamous crime is an exciting game, a means to gaining the media spotlight, or perhaps just a way to say what the authorities seem to want them to say. Reliance upon the accuracy of such confessions can and does mislead all of the primary actors.

A final category of means of reducing the execution of the innocent would be to replace the emphasis on winning with an emphasis on accuracy. Litigators, both at trial and on appeal, want to win, sometimes at all costs. In the field of criminal law generally, one does not always witness the highest of ethical behavior. In death penalty cases, played out in the media spotlight for the highest stakes, the desire to win may result in even more questionable behavior by both sides. Prosecutors see themselves as fighting crime in their community, and defense attorneys see themselves as fighting to save their client's life. Both sides tend to become camps of true believers, highly derogatory of "the enemy" and in no mood to cooperate and to work toward a just result. For the defense attorney, this ultimate advocacy role is a result in large part of the 6th Amendment requirement that the defense attorney provide effective assistance of counsel. The defense attorney's nearly sole obligation is to serve the interests of the client. Rarely would this entail the defense attorney's knowingly or even inadvertently getting a death sentence for a client who in fact is innocent.

In contrast to the role of the defense attorney, the prosecutor takes an oath to "seek justice" as well as to serve as an advocate for the state. Presumably all would agree that putting an innocent person on death row would not be "justice" and thus should be avoided at all costs by the prosecutor. Beyond these standard roles, many prosecutors see themselves as the personal attorneys for the victim's family, as if this were a wrongful death lawsuit in civil court. It is not unusual for the victim's family members to be extremely distraught over the murder of their family member, to have focused their all-consuming hatred for whomever did this upon the defendant in this case, and to want more than anything for that defendant to be sentenced to death as "justice" for the deceased. Indeed, when a death sentence is not returned, members of the victim's family often express their disappointment at the outcome. To the degree that the prosecutor takes on this additional and improper role of private counsel for the victim's family, the prosecutor may tend to seek the goals of those "clients." If those goals include the death of the defendant, the desire to achieve that goal may cloud the other authorized roles of the prosecutor to represent the state and to seek justice.

We cannot expect to change the American criminal justice process from a nearly no-holds-barred adversarial system to more of an inquisitorial system by pointing out these problems and suggested solutions. No one expects these seasoned warriors to lay down their weapons quickly and come to the discussion table. Indeed, many constitutional law provisions would make that quite difficult to accomplish. This discussion might begin to lead the way, however, to lessening the pressure and asking all players to focus less on winning and more on avoiding executing the innocent.

CHAPTER 18

FOREIGN AND INTERNATIONAL LAW ISSUES

The American death penalty system does not exist in a vacuum. First, the criminal justice systems of other countries, particularly as to their use of the death penalty, provide the global context in which the American death penalty system operates. With what countries are we in step in this regard, and what countries might find us out of step? In addition to the subtle and informal pressures of the death penalty practices of our neighbors and allies around the world, the United States also is a party to and is bound by international treaties and other agreements concerning the death penalty. International courts hand down rulings on American death penalty cases as well. Should the United States continue to ignore this body of international law as to the death penalty? As we continually measure those elusive "evolving standards of decency that mark the progress of a maturing society" in order to determine if the 8th Amendment prohibits a specific aspect of the death penalty, should foreign and international law be a part of the measurement?

§ 18.1 Death Penalty in Foreign Countries

As described briefly in § 1.1, the death penalty has an extensive, worldwide history, dating back to our earliest records of civilizations. However, beginning in the mid–19th century, a movement to abolish the death penalty got underway. This movement persisted continually, but a century passed without much progress. A 1965 report to the United Nations noted that only 12 countries had abolished the death penalty completely, with another 11 countries having abolished it for ordinary crimes during peacetime. Actual implementation of the death penalty certainly had fallen out of favor in most countries, but formal governmental action to abolish it had seldom kept pace with the actual practice.

The latter third of the 20th century saw an ever-increasing number of countries formally reject the death penalty, either by constitutional amendment, by statutory amendment, or by high court ruling. During this period, 58 additional countries abolished the death penalty (46 totally and 12 for ordinary crimes). Many additional countries simply stopped using the death penalty without formal legal action, making them de facto abolitionist countries. This increased pace of countries abolishing the death penalty has continued into the early 21st century as well. In this period of political turmoil, countries come and go, split and merge, so the exact count of what country has what death penalty policy is never quite certain. However, our world continues to have about 200 independent countries, and the continuing evolution away from the death penalty is clear.

A survey as of January 2008 found that the worldwide status of the death penalty was as follows:

abolitionist for all crimes:	91
abolitionist for ordinary crimes only:	11
abolitionist de facto:	33
Total abolitionist in law or practice:	135
Countries retaining the death penalty:	63

The Council of Europe, a strong opponent of the death penalty, has discarded even its wartime exception to this policy. Any country wishing to become or remain a member of the Council of Europe is required to abolish the death penalty, and this has provided the final push for European countries to exact formal legislation doing so.

As of the end of 2007, less than one-third of the 200 countries in the world still authorized the death penalty. Europe and Latin America have abolished the death penalty, while the Middle East and Asia still retain it. World-wide executions have been decreasing, with 2,188 in 2005, 1,591 in 2006, and 1,252 in 2007. The leading country for many years is China, with 470 executions just in 2007. Next in line in 2007 were Iran with 317 executions, Saudi Arabia with 143, Pakistan with 135, and the United States with 42. These top five countries accounted for 88% of the executions worldwide in 2007. Another 19 countries also executed prisoners, but typically only a handful of executions were imposed in each of them.

In sum, only 24 (38%) of the 63 countries that officially authorized the death penalty in 2007 were actually executing prisoners. China's 470 executions in 2007 were by far the most, but China had 1,010 executions in 2006 and 1,770 executions in 2005. Although declining dramatically in annual executions, China nonetheless has remained the leader with Iran steadily in second place, followed variously by Saudi Arabia, Pakistan, Iraq and the United States. Observers have noted that these are odd bedfellows for the United States. At a minimum, it is true that we seldom look to China and countries in the Middle East when seeking positive role models for the fundamental legal and moral policies of American society. In fact, no country anything at all like the United States has continued to execute prisoners into the 21st century.

Within the general practice of executing prisoners, the specific issues of executing juvenile and mentally retarded offenders have been fairly unique. Reliable data as to execution of the mentally retarded are seldom available, primarily because accurate testing of capital defendants and death row prisoners has seldom been commonplace. However, it does seem clear that "within the world community, the imposition of the death penalty for crimes committed by mentally retarded offenders is overwhelmingly disapproved." *Atkins v. Virginia*, 536 U.S. 304, 122 S.Ct. 2242, 153 L.Ed.2d 335 (2002). This disapproval also is apparently shared by widely diverse religious communities reflecting Christian, Jewish, Muslim, and Buddhist traditions. Nonetheless, during the 1989–2002 time period, the United States executed at least five mentally retarded offenders in Alabama, Louisiana, South Carolina, Texas, and Virginia. The *Atkins* ruling relied in part upon this worldwide disapproval and very small number of United States executions to find the death penalty for the mentally retarded to be unconstitutional.

Considerably more accurate data have been collected for the execution of juvenile offenders (those who committed their crimes while under the age of 18). Amnesty International documented executions of juvenile offenders in eight countries (including the United States) from 1985 through 2000, and it is reasonable to assume that other such executions occurred but have not been or cannot be documented. Perhaps the most shocking of these was the case of Nasser Munir Nasser al'Kirbi in Yemen. He was only 13 years old when he was executed on July 21, 1993.

Meanwhile, the United States executed 22 juvenile offenders from 1985 through 2003, by far the most of any country in the world. All but one of these juvenile offenders were age 17 at crime, with Sean Sellers being only age 16 at the time of his crime in Oklahoma. The extreme rarity of the death penalty for juvenile offenders in foreign countries has not been lost on the Supreme Court. *Thompson v. Oklahoma*, 487 U.S. 815, 108 S.Ct. 2687, 101 L.Ed.2d 702 (1988) expressly considered the views held "by other nations that share our Anglo–American heritage, and by the leading members of the

Western European community" in rejecting the death penalty for 15–year-old offenders. By the early 21st century, the death penalty for all offenders under the age of 18 had disappeared everywhere in the world except in the United States. The Supreme Court finally put an end to this practice in *Roper v. Simmons*, 543 U.S. 551, 125 S.Ct. 1183, 161 L.Ed.2d 1 (2005), relying in part upon this international climate.

§ 18.2 Treaties and Other International Agreements

The fact that the United States is essentially the only country in all of the western hemisphere and Europe that continues to implement the death penalty puts considerable informal pressure on us from our friends and allies abroad. However, much more forceful than any "informal pressure" is the impact of treaties. According to the Article VI, clause 2, of the United States Constitution, the "supreme law of the land" is based on the Constitution, laws and treaties of the United States. If this provision is taken literally, United States treaties are just as binding upon our death penalty system as is any other major provision of our law. Therefore, it is not surprising that some death penalty defendants rely on provisions of international law at trial, on appeal, and throughout the death penalty process. This reliance seems particularly on point in federal habeas corpus proceedings, in that the federal statute expressly provides that relief may be granted to petitioners who are "in custody in violation of the

Constitution or laws or treaties of the United States." 28 U.S.C. § 2254(a).

Many international treaties and agreements, such as the International Covenant on Civil and Political Rights ("ICCPR"), expressly prohibit "cruel, inhuman or degrading treatment or punishment." This provision was interpreted in 1982 by the United Nations Human Rights Committee as including the notion that "all measures of abolition should be considered as progress in the enjoyment of the right to life." These and similar comments have led many to interpret this provision of the ICCPR as encouraging the reduction and abolition of the death penalty, certainly not its expansion.

The United States ratified the ICCPR in 1992 but entered many reservations to its various provisions, including the stipulation that "cruel, inhuman or degrading treatment or punishment" is to be defined by punishments acceptable or unacceptable under the 5th, 8th, and 14th Amendments to the United States Constitution. This reservation, obviously, was meant to avoid any need to alter American death penalty law to fit the confines of international law. As recently as 1998, President Clinton issued an executive order declaring that it "shall be the policy and practice of the Government of the United States, being committed to the protection and promotion of human rights and fundamental freedoms, fully to respect and implement its obligations under the international human rights treaties to which it is a party, including the ICCPR [and others]." This 1998 executive order, just as the

1992 ratification, had no apparent impact upon the death penalty system.

More focused than the sweeping "right to life" provisions commonly found in international documents, several other international treaties and agreements specifically establish a minimum age of 18 for capital punishment. Since at least the end of World War II, the juvenile death penalty has been prohibited by several prominent international documents. Among the best known and most highly respected is the Geneva Convention. For example, the Geneva Convention Relative to the Protection of Civilian Persons in Time of War (1949) provides: "In any case, the death penalty may not be pronounced on a protected person who was less than eighteen years of age at the time of the offense." More recent provisions include the ICCPR, entered into force in 1976, ("Sentence of death shall not be imposed for crimes committed by persons below eighteen years of age . . ."), and the American Convention on Human Rights, entered into force in 1978 ("Capital punishment shall not be imposed upon persons who, at the time the crime was committed, were under 18 years of age . . .").

Dominating this international issue during the current death penalty era has been the United Nations Convention on the Rights of the Child ("Convention"). Article 37(a) of the Convention provides: "Neither capital punishment nor life imprisonment without possibility of release shall be imposed for offences committed by persons below eighteen years of age." Echoing treaty provisions for over half a century, this is not vague reference to cruel punishment or a right to life. The Convention flatly prohibits the death penalty for juvenile offenders. As of the early 21st century, all but one of the nearly 200 functioning nations of the world have ratified the Convention, making it the most widely-approved international treaty in history. The one nation that has not ratified the Convention is the United States. It was signed by our President but has not been ratified by the United States Senate, and few have realistic hopes that ratification will ever occur. Meanwhile, as described in § 7.2 and § 18.1, the United States was by far the world leader in the execution of juvenile offenders.

In a world in which all nations except one subscribed to the principle of excluding the juvenile death penalty, an argument can be made that this principle establishes an ethical norm with the weight of international consensus that preempts all contrary norms, including contrary treaty provisions. This is a form of international common law, often labeled jus cogens, and it must be obeyed even by countries that have not ratified treaties establishing this principle of international law. As of the Supreme Court's decision in *Roper v. Simmons*, 543 U.S. 551, 125 S.Ct. 1183, 161 L.Ed.2d 1 (2005), this argument has begun to be persuasive before American legislatures and judicial bodies.

Similarly focused provisions on other specific death penalty issues can be found in international law. For example, condemned prisoners in the United States spend an average of about nine years on death row prior to execution, and many spend well over twice that long. The ICCPR prohibition, among others, of "cruel, inhuman or degrading treatment or punishment" would seem to include such extended incarceration on death row. Although several death row prisoners have raised this international law issue, it has not yet been successful in our state or federal courts.

The problem of race bias within the American death penalty system (see § 16.1) raises yet another specific international law issue. The International Convention on the Elimination of All Forms of Racial Discrimination ("ICERD") was ratified by the United States Senate in 1994. Article 2.1(c) provides: "Each State Party shall take effective measures to review governmental, national and local policies, and to amend, rescind or nullify any laws and regulations which have the effect of creating or perpetuating racial discrimination wherever it exists." Does ICERD directly contradict the holding of *McCleskey v. Kemp*, 481 U.S. 279, 107 S.Ct. 1756, 95 L.Ed.2d 262 (1987) and/or does it require the enactment of Racial Justice Acts (see § 16.1)? As with other international treaties and agreements, death penalty challenges based upon ICERD have not been successful.

A final specific example is the execution of foreign nationals by the American death penalty system. These are situations in which a citizen of a foreign country is in the United States and commits a capital crime. That foreign national is then processed, typically, through the state death penalty system and can end up being executed by those state authorities. The Vienna Convention, ratified by the United States in 1969, provides that governmental officials who arrest a foreign national must inform the arrestee of his right to consult with the embassy of the arrestee's home country. The benefits to the foreign national include notification to his family and friends back home and access to any support they or his home government might be able to provide during the death penalty process. Americans abroad routinely expect and receive such embassy notification, and foreign nationals in the United States have similar rights.

A large number of cases have been discovered in which this provision of the Vienna Convention has simply been ignored by state officials arresting, trying, and executing foreign nationals. Despite the clarity of the right and the undeniability of the violation of that right, this issue has not yet been the basis for overturning a death sentence. A citizen of Paraguay was executed in 1998 for a crime committed in Virginia, after the Supreme Court denied him relief on procedural grounds. *Breard v. Greene*, 523 U.S. 371, 118 S.Ct. 1352, 140 L.Ed.2d 529 (1998). Two German citizens were executed in 1999 in Arizona, with the Supreme Court deciding that both Arizona and the United States were immune from suit. *Federal Republic of Germany v. United States*, 526 U.S. 111, 119 S.Ct. 1016, 143 L.Ed.2d 192 (1999).

In March of 2004, the International Court of Justice determined in the *Avena* case (Mexico v. USA) that advisement of consular rights "without delay" means "a duty upon the arresting authorities to give that information to an arrested person as soon as it is realized that the person is a foreign national, or once there are grounds to think that the person is probably a foreign national." In most cases, arresting police in the United States would become aware of a suspect's probable nationality through routine identity confirmation and computerized background checks, done either prior to arrest, during the arrest or very shortly thereafter. The State Department has in the past interpreted the term "without delay" to mean as soon as practicable (*i.e.* without undue delay) and normally by the time the detainee is booked for detention, but that advisement upon arraignment in court would also meet this requirement. While not all of the reported foreign nationals currently on death row were deprived of their consular rights by arresting authorities, there is overwhelming evidence that prompt notification of these rights across the United States remains highly sporadic. No comparative study has yet been done, but the available data indicates that timely consular assistance significantly reduces the likelihood that death sentences will be sought or imposed on foreign nationals facing capital charges.

Even applying the less stringent definition of prompt notification used by the State Department, only seven cases of complete compliance with Article 36 requirements have been identified so far, out of more than 160 total reported death sentences (including those executed, reversed on appeal or released). In most of the remaining cases, detained nationals learned of their consular rights weeks, months or even years after their arrest, typically from attorneys or other prisoners and not from the local authorities. As a consequence, consular officials were often unable to provide crucial assistance to their nationals when it would be most beneficial: at the arrest and pre-trial stage of capital cases. For example, Arizona authorities did not formally inform German nationals Karl and Walter LaGrand of their Article 36 rights until 17 years after their arrest—and just weeks before their execution.

Jose Medellin is a Mexican citizen who has been on Texas' death row since 1993. After the International Court of Justice ruling in 2004, Texas refused to review Medellin's case, and he petitioned the Supreme Court for relief. In the meantime, President Bush ordered the respective state courts to provide the review required by the International Court of Justice. Texas courts again refused to grant such a review, claiming that President Bush did not have the power to give such an order, so Medellin appealed to the Supreme Court for a second time. The Bush administration's brief noted that the Texas court's decision, if not reversed, "will place the United States in breach of its international law obligation" to comply with the World Court's decision and would "frustrate the president's judgment that foreign policy interests are best served by giving effect to that decision." On March 25, 2008, the Supreme Court ruled 6–3 in *Medellin v. Texas*, ___ U.S. ___, 128 S.Ct. 1346, 170 L.Ed.2d 190 (2008) that the President does not have the authority to order states to bypass their procedural rules and comply with a ruling from the International Court of Justice. As of this writing, Texas has set Medellin's execution for August 5, 2008.

§ 18.3   United States Response to International Pressures

As with most areas of law, political eras come and go, and being in step with other nations goes in and out of fashion. The United States vacillates between building coalitions of allies for international efforts against terrorism, and going it alone in other situations. The importance of foreign and international law on the death penalty meets with similarly mixed reviews, according to the time period and to the politics of the reviewer. Nonetheless, this issue continues in court arguments and decisions, legislative debates, clemency considerations, and even international relations. The fact that the United States is nearly alone as a death penalty nation among its friends and allies in the world is always an issue, sometimes subtle and sometimes express, but always there.

The solely intra-national issue is whether foreign and international law should impact the power of the United States to impose the death penalty. The inclusion in the United States Constitution of treaties among those authorities which are the supreme law of the land has not yet shunted aside the death penalty. In several cases, this is because the United States has entered reservations to the pertinent parts of the treaty before ratifying it, thereby either excluding the death penalty restrictions from the treaty or, perhaps, rendering invalid our ratification of the entire treaty. See, *e.g.*, *Domingues v. State*, 961 P.2d 1279 (Nev.1998). Nonetheless, these several treaties and international agreements, along with jus cogens or international common law, provide a backdrop against which our domestic death penalty laws are to be viewed.

The other intra-national issue is whether the laws and practices of foreign countries should be part of the consideration of the "evolving standards of decency" in 8th Amendment law. On this issue, our courts have been strongly divided. Passing reference has been made, however, to "the climate of international opinion" in considering the appropriateness of the death penalty. *Coker v. Georgia*, 433 U.S. 584, 97 S.Ct. 2861, 53 L.Ed.2d 982 (1977). In the original case which gave birth to the evolving standards of decency test, Chief Justice Warren's four-justice plurality opinion expressly looked to the practices of the "civilized nations of the world" in determining 8th Amendment law. *Trop v. Dulles*, 356 U.S. 86, 78 S.Ct. 590, 2 L.Ed.2d 630 (1958). In *Thompson v. Oklahoma*, 487 U.S. 815, 108 S.Ct. 2687, 101 L.Ed.2d.702 (1988), Justice Stevens' four-justice plurality opinion included the laws and practices of "other nations that share our Anglo–American heritage, and ... the leading members of the Western European community" in the calculus of whether the death penalty for fifteen-year-old offenders was cruel and unusual under the 8th

Amendment. The next year, Justice Scalia's four-justice plurality opinion in *Stanford v. Kentucky*, 492 U.S. 361, 109 S.Ct. 2969, 106 L.Ed.2d 306 (1989) emphatically noted that only "*American* conceptions of decency ... are dispositive" in measuring evolving standards of decency (emphasis in original).

In *Atkins v. Virginia*, 536 U.S. 304, 122 S.Ct. 2242, 153 L.Ed.2d 335 (2002), members of the Supreme Court continued their disagreement. Justice Stevens' six-justice majority opinion in *Atkins*, holding that a national consensus has developed against the death penalty for the mentally retarded, expressly relied upon the laws and practices of "the world community" as "further support of our conclusion that there is a consensus among those who have addressed the issue." Chief Justice Rehnquist dissented (along with Justices Scalia and Thomas) in *Atkins*, observing that "if it is evidence of a *national* consensus for which we are looking, then the viewpoints of other countries simply are not relevant" (emphasis in original). Noting that the four-justice plurality in *Trop* had considered foreign and international law, Chief Justice Rehnquist referred to the "sound rejection" of that argument by the four-justice plurality in *Stanford*. He does not explain how a four-justice plurality opinion can provide a "sound rejection" of another four-justice plurality opinion. In contrast, the six-justice majority opinion in *Atkins* expressly relies upon this factor, leaving a divided Supreme Court but with a two-thirds majority willing at least to consider foreign and international law in 8th Amendment decisions.

A recent development in this ongoing dispute is *Roper v. Simmons*, 543 U.S. 551, 125 S.Ct. 1183, 161 L.Ed.2d 1 (2005). Justice Kennedy's majority opinion in *Simmons* relies even more strongly on international and comparative law in determining the evolving standards of decency under the 8th Amendment to the United States Constitution. The same three dissenters (Scalia, Rehnquist, and Thomas) have not changed their mind, but a majority of the Court fairly consistently supports Justice Kennedy's position.

Formal legal rulings from outside of the United States seem to have little impact upon domestic death penalty cases. A long string of American death sentences and pending executions have been condemned and "overruled" by a variety of international and agencies, resting their decisions both upon international treaties and agreements and upon jus cogens or international common law. The orders resulting from these rulings have been aimed at overturning a death sentence or forbidding an execution. As of the early 21st century, no American court, governor, or president has felt bound by such decisions in death penalty cases, but several signs indicate that this may be changing.

Informal political pressures in the international arena are even more common than formal pressures, and they tend to have some effect in selected cases. Perhaps the best-known incident was the clemency granted to a death row prisoner by the Governor of Missouri when the Pope visited there and made a personal request concerning that pending execution. The Vatican regularly requests stays and clemency in pending executions, but rarely do its requests appear to be persuasive. Considerable pressure from a wide variety of international human rights organizations is being brought to bear on the United States around this issue, but American death penalty states seem even less interested in their views. A fairly common reaction has been for proud and independent states (*e.g.*, Texas) to loudly proclaim that "foreign outsiders" will not dictate to them what to do in death penalty cases. One sees a particularly negative view toward intervention by the United Nations.

Sometimes more formal international relations are impacted negatively by domestic death penalty decisions. For example, in August 2002, Texas executed a Mexican national, sentenced to death for a murder committed in Texas, over the repeated objections of President Fox of Mexico. President Fox promptly canceled his scheduled trip to meet with President Bush in Texas to discuss a variety of issues. This illustrates that even such a close alliance as that between Mexico and the United States and between Presidents Fox and Bush can be chilled by an isolated, state-level death penalty case. Other examples include the refusal of foreign courts to authorize extradition of alleged murderers sought by the United States unless we provide assurances that the death penalty will not be imposed. In an era of international terrorists inflicting unthinkable mass murder on American soil, whether or not we can get them into American courts is of great importance to us. Ironically, the price of gaining this personal jurisdiction over them may be foregoing the possibility of the death penalty for the worst murderers in American history.

The net impact of the international community may be felt more around the edges of the American death penalty. As described in § 18.2, international condemnation was particularly strong in death penalty cases involving juvenile offenders and foreign nationals. As apparently the only country in the world which was still executing juvenile offenders, the United States continued to make unflattering international news in these cases. With 123 foreign nationals on death row in 2008, we also hear from the countries in which these persons hold citizenship. Our continuing to disregard the clear requirements of the Vienna Convention in these cases seemed difficult to explain to these other countries. In these two areas particularly, it appears that international pressure plays a role in bringing change to the American death penalty system.

As the world community continues to move toward total abolition of all death penalties, the United States can expect to continue to be seen as out of step with the 21st century. The fact that every other country in the world anything like the United States has now abandoned the death penalty is a serious issue of international relations for us. How can we continue to exert a leadership position as to international human rights when this high-profile human rights issue is regularly thrown in our face? Increasingly, the United States is being portrayed as a human rights violator by nations we consider to be our friends and allies.

POSTSCRIPT

FUTURE OF THE DEATH PENALTY

If actual executions are such rare occurrences, why the enormous amount of political discussion, media coverage, and social angst over the death penalty? For urban areas seeing thousands of innocent victims of homicide each year, why should we care about a few guilty murderers being executed each year? The reasons for the continuing commentary and debate include its usefulness to our media-fed hysteria about crime, our changing social order, and our need to "send a message" to all of the real and imagined sources of our fears.

This leads us to the obvious questions about whether the death penalty "works" or not. It clearly doesn't work if this means reducing our homicide rate. Research findings over generations of studies have made it clear that the death penalty is not a greater general deterrent to homicide than is its alternative, long-term imprisonment. Particularly troubling findings of this research indicate that the death penalty may result in a higher homicide rate than imprisonment would, that capital punishment apparently stimulates more homicides. This is true at least in part because government-approved kill-

ing of undesirables encourages homicidal individuals to kill people they find undesirable.

But what of the real world of the death penalty?
What lies beyond the holier-than-thou rhetoric from
both sides of the debate over the jurisprudential
principle of capital punishment? Confronting the
stench of this real world system causes even the
strongest death penalty proponent to gag. Even if
certain offenders "deserve to die," can we continue
a governmental system of death so terribly biased
along unacceptable lines? Knowing that government
programs often make mistakes, how many executions of innocent persons can we tolerate in order to
maintain this system? What actually happens is
considerably messier than the lofty, scholarly debate over death penalty jurisprudence.

From the earliest executions in our colonial period, these same truths have plagued the death penalty. Completely separate from the crime, additional
key factors determining who lives and who dies
have always included the race, class, religion, and
sex of the offender and victim. Despite all of our
efforts to remove these biases from the system, they
remain today much as they always have been. Consider the poor black Muslim male who kills the
middle class white Christian female and is represented by a poorly paid, ill-prepared defense attorney. He is the defendant most likely to be executed.

While there are those who think the real world
death penalty system discriminates in ways that are
fine, even most of those strongly in favor of the idea

of the death penalty don't want it to continue to be so biased. Our courts, and to a lesser degree our legislatures, have made a variety of changes to reduce these flaws but to no avail. The bottom line is that the real world death penalty system, in the light of day, discriminates grossly based on the race, class, and sex of the offender and victim. It always has been so, in the United States and every other country in which it has been used.

For the first time since the 1960s, the United States appears to be having second thoughts about the death penalty. Public opinion surveys which had shown about 80% support in 1994 were down significantly to 65% in 2006. When more sophisticated questions are posed, providing a choice between the death penalty or life imprisonment for murder, 47% favor the death penalty and 48% favor life imprisonment.

In political campaigns, the positions of candidates on the death penalty are once again being investigated. It must be said that almost all candidates say they favor the death penalty, but until recently this issue was not even seen as worthy of consideration. The American Bar Association has called for a moratorium on executions until some of the more serious problems with the system can be worked out. Illinois and Maryland have adopted moratoriums, with Illinois particularly concerned about execution of the innocent and Maryland particularly interested in racial disparity issues. Many other states, as well as the federal government, are considering moratoriums as well. The death sentencing rate has dropped from about 320 per year in the mid–1990s to about one-third that rate in the early 21st century. Actual executions peaked in 1999 at 98, with only 53 in 2006 and 42 in 2007.

Recent developments may have provided the last straw. Given our experience with government-run programs, we just know that mistakes will be fairly common. The mistake we fear most in the death penalty system is getting the wrong guy—executing an innocent person. Research has uncovered an ever-growing list of such fatal errors, with over 125 persons released from death row as of the early 21st century because they were found to be innocent. If we could have blind faith that death penalty errors almost never occurred, we might endorse both the principle and the practice of the death penalty. Now even the strongest proponents of the principle of the death penalty for the worst of the worst murderers are concerned about mistaken execution of the innocent.

It appears that the American death penalty is in its final stages—in its death throes, if you will. Every other society anything like ours has already relegated the death penalty to history, and now they look back to us, wondering when we will step into the modern world. Cracks in the foundation of support for the death penalty are clearly evident, and few seem to have much eagerness to repair the cracks and to undergird the death penalty system. It is likely to fade slowly, to go out with a whimper and not a bang. This nearly happened in the late 1960s when executions simply stopped, essentially from disinterest and not from major revisions in law or policy. The system reared up again in the 1970s for one last hurrah, and now it appears to be fading for good. As it does, the United States may once again be welcomed as a full-fledged member of the international community of human rights.

*

INDEX

References are to Pages

EXECUTION—Cont'd
Time elapsing between sentencing and execution, 7, 125
Witnesses, 127

EXPENSE OF DEATH PENALTY
Arguments for and against death penalty, 24

EYE FOR AN EYE
Arguments for and against death penalty, 12, 13

EYEWITNESSES
Execution of innocent persons, 262, 274

FAMILIES
Domestic homicide, this index
Victim's family, this index

FELONY-MURDER
Aggravating circumstances, 73, 83, 84, 92
Class of offenders for death penalty, 68–70
Defined, 61

FIRST-TIME OFFENDERS
Criminal record, this index

FOREIGN AND INTERNATIONAL LAW ISSUES
    Generally, 277–296
Commission of capital crime by foreign national, 294, 295
Death penalty in foreign countries, 278–282
Future of death penalty in US, 297–301
International pressures, US response to, 290–296
Juvenile offenders, this index
Supreme law of land, treaties as, 282, 283, 290, 291
Treaties and agreements, generally, 282–290
United Nations, this index

FUTURE OF DEATH PENALTY
Postscript discussing, 297–301

GAY PERSONS
Sexual orientation, this index

GENDER BIAS
    Generally, 18, 19, 249, 254–258
Aggravating and mitigating circumstances, 78, 94–96, 256, 257
Arguments for and against death penalty, 18, 19
Due process and equal protection, aggravating circumstances
    that violate, 78

VICTIMS
Family. Victim's family, this index
Respect for victim's life as argument for death penalty, 22, 23
Valuable victim cases, 92
Victim Impact Statement (VIS), 165–169

VIENNA CONVENTION
Foreign and international law issues, 287, 288, 295, 296

WEALTH
Socioeconomic status, this index

WITNESSES
Evidence, this index
Execution, witnesses to, 127, 225
Eyewitness testimony and execution of innocent persons, 262, 263

†